MAKING
WOODEN
MECHANICAL
MODELS

ALAN AND GILL BRIDGEWATER

BETTERWAY BOOKS

CINCINNATI, OHIO

Disclaimer

To prevent accidents, keep safety in mind while you work. Use the safety guards installed on power equipment; they are for your protection. When working on power equipment, keep fingers away from saw blades, wear safety goggles to prevent injuries from flying wood chips and sawdust, wear headphones to protect your hearing, and consider installing a dust vacuum to reduce the amount of airborne sawdust in your woodshop. Don't wear loose clothing, such as neckties or shirts with loose sleeves, or jewelry, such as rings, necklaces or bracelets, when working on power equipment, and tie back long hair to prevent it from getting caught in your equipment.

The authors and editors who compiled this book have tried to make all the contents as accurate and correct as possible. Plans, illustrations, photographs and text have been carefully checked. All instructions, plans and projects should be carefully read, studied and understood before beginning construction. Due to the variability of local conditions, construction materials, skill levels, etc., neither the authors nor Betterway Books assumes any responsibility for any accidents, injuries, damages or other losses incurred resulting from the material presented in this book.

Library of Congress Cataloging-in-Publication Data

Bridgewater, Alan.
    Making wooden mechanical models : 15 designs with visible wheels, cranks, pistons, cogs, and cams / Alan and Gill Bridgewater.—1st ed.
        p.   cm.
Includes index.
ISBN 1-55870-381-0 (pb : alk. paper)
1. Woodwork. 2. Machinery—Models. 3. Models and modelmaking. I. Bridgewater, Gill. II. Title.
TT185.B738   1995
621.8'0228—dc20
                                                95-14143
                                                    CIP

Editor: R. Adam Blake
Production editor: Bob Beckstead
Interior designer: Angela Lennert
Cover designer: Brian Roeth

METRIC CONVERSION CHART		
TO CONVERT	**TO**	**MULTIPLY BY**
Inches	Centimeters	2.54
Centimeters	Inches	0.4
Feet	Centimeters	30.5
Centimeters	Feet	0.03
Yards	Meters	0.9
Meters	Yards	1.1
Sq. Inches	Sq. Centimeters	6.45
Sq. Centimeters	Sq. Inches	0.16
Sq. Feet	Sq. Meters	0.09
Sq. Meters	Sq. Feet	10.8
Sq. Yards	Sq. Meters	0.8
Sq. Meters	Sq. Yards	1.2
Pounds	Kilograms	0.45
Kilograms	Pounds	2.2
Ounces	Grams	28.4

DEDICATION

We would like to dedicate this book to all the men and women of the past—inventors, engineers, clockmakers and the like—who spent countless hours in workshops making little machines and working models in wood. We all know about Leonardo da Vinci and his helicopter, and Stevenson and his loco, but who was it I wonder who made the first working model for say, the first padlock? Or the first pair of roller skates?

ACKNOWLEDGMENTS

We would like to thank all the manufacturers who have supplied us with the best of the best:

Tim Effrem, President, Wood Carvers Supply
P.O. Box 7500
Englewood FL 34295-7500
Wood Carving Tools

Jim Brewer, Research and Marketing Manager, Freud
P.O. Box 7187, 218 Feld Ave.
High Point NC 27264
Forstner Drill Bits

William Nelsen, President, Foredom Electric
Bethel CT 06801
Power Tools

John P. Jodkin, Vice President, Delta International
    Machinery Corp.
246 Alpha Dr.
Pittsburgh PA 15238-2985
Band Saw

Nick Davidson, Managing Director, Craft Supplies Ltd UK
The Mill
Millers Dale
Buxton, Derbyshire, SK17 8SN UK
Wood for Turning

Dawn Fretz, Marketing Assistant, De-Sta-Co
P.O. Box 2800
Troy MI 48007
Clamps

Paragon Communications, Evo-Stick
Common Road
Stafford, ST16 3EH UK
PVA Adhesive

Frank Cootz, Public Relations, Ryobi America
    Corporation
5201 Pearman Dairy Rd., Suite 1
P.O. Box 1207
Anderson SC 29622-1207
Thickness Planer

TABLE OF CONTENTS

CIRCULAR MOVEMENT MACHINE

FLYWHEEL PROPELLER MACHINE

OIL PUMPING RIG

PENDULUM RECOIL ESCAPEMENT MACHINE

IN-THE-ROUND COMBUSTION ENGINE

RACK AND PINION MACHINE

RECIPROCATING ENGINE

HARMONIC OSCILLATION PUNCH MACHINE

WARD LOCK AND KEY

FLYWHEEL AND GOVERNOR MACHINE

CAM MACHINE

CAM AND FORK MACHINE

SECTOR WHEEL BEARING MACHINE

CENTRIFUGAL IMPELLER PUMP

PYRAMID ROLLER-BALL MACHINE

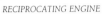

INTRODUCTION

When I was a child—I must have been about eight years old—I was forever trying to make some sort of weird and wonderful wooden machine or other. One time it was a very complicated and slightly dangerous weight-wheel-and-see-saw mechanism that linked my alarm clock to the bedside lamp, and then another time it was a catch on the shed door that was operated by the weight of the person approaching the shed, and so the list goes on. Well, of course, when I now look back, I see that my interests were twofold: On the one hand, I enjoyed playing around with mechanisms—weights, levers, wheels and the like—and on the other hand, I simply enjoyed the pleasures of handling and shaping wood.

The intention of this book is to explore and demonstrate the use of all the skills and techniques involved in producing what might best be described as key mechanisms and machines in wood. Machines made from wood? OK, so in many ways it might be thought that wood and machinery make for an odd couple, but that's not so. History tells us that if we could go back in time to, say, Leonardo da Vinci's workshop, Galileo's observatory, Benjamin Franklin's laboratory, Samuel Colt's gunmaking workshop, Isambard Kingdom Brunel's shipyards or wherever, we would almost certainly see people beavering away variously whittling, sawing, shaping wood, and making small-scale working mechanisms and machines.

Occasionally, when I am comfortably ensconced in my small, cozy workshop—with the sun shining through the window, my dog dozing on a pile of wood shavings, and my tools and piles of timber surrounding me—I take one or other of my little wooden machines and spend time running my eyes and fingertips over its forms and textures—it's an amazingly satisfying feeling! To see the way the grain flows through the structure; to wonder as the light catches the colors within the wood; to marvel at the characteristics of the various wooden component parts that make up the project—say a piece of silky, butter-colored lime or maybe a piece of plum with its deep, rich, honey-brown hues—to study the way the wooden components link, relate and operate one to another; and then to remember the many happy hands-on hours spent cutting, shaping and working with wood—these are, without doubt, uniquely beautiful experiences that should not be missed.

The intention, or you might say ambitions, of this book involves sharing with you all the pure playtime pleasures of building and creating small machines and mechanical prototypes from wood. With each and every project, we take you through the procedures of drawing out the designs, of making decisions as to the best type of wood to use for the task in hand, and of choosing the best tools for the job. We tell you how to use the tools and machines, we show you with scaled, gridded working drawings what goes where and how, we illustrate with photographs and pen drawings how best to achieve such and such a cut; in fact, we take you through all the stages of designing, making, constructing and finishing. We do our level best to describe all the procedures that go into making our working wooden wonders.

Each project relates to or is inspired by a specific mechanism or machine. There are such juicy delights as a circular movement machine, a pendulum recoil escapement machine, and a flywheel and governor machine. There are fifteen projects in all.

Making Wooden Mechanical Models does not require a workshop full of complex and expensive tools or shelves stacked high with rare and exotic woods (our wish is that you only use renewable species); it requires only that you become involved in the close, physically satisfying and therapeutic experience of working with wood—our most beautiful natural material.

Making Wooden Mechanical Models is about personal involvement, working with your hands, and the joy and pleasure of using your mind and body to create uniquely beautiful machines in wood. What else to say except "Best of Luck!"

TOOLS & MATERIALS

- Scroll saw.
- Band saw.
- Bench drill.
- Forstner drill bits.
- Rotary power tool.
- Small drum sander.
- Pencil and ruler.
- Back saw.
- Pair of compasses or dividers.
- Sharp whittling knife.
- Adjustable angle square.
- Lathe.
- Good selection of lathe tools.
- Four-jaw chuck to fit your lathe.
- Screw chuck to fit your lathe.
- Tailstock drill chuck.
- Tracing paper.
- Teak oil.
- The usual workshop tools and materials—sandpaper, calipers, dividers, etc.
- Good selection of clamps.

PROJECT ONE

Circular Movement Machine

Color photo page 27

PROJECT BACKGROUND

This machine is amazingly interesting in that it beautifully illustrates one of the key principles of horology. It shows how, in the context of a traditional grandfather-type clock, a pulley drum, length of cord and weight are able—like a coiled spring—to store up and provide energy.

The movement is handsomely direct and uncomplicated. As the weight falls at a constant rate, so the drum-and-beam flywheel spins at a uniform speed on its pivot. The fascinating thing is that the position of the pill weights on the beam dramatically alters the speed of spin.

To set the machine into motion, the cord is wound up with the crank handle, the two flywheel weights are adjusted so they are equidistant from the center of spin, and the weight is allowed to descend. If you have a yen to play around with flywheels, crank handles and pulley weights, and if you enjoy a good working mix of wood turning, fretting on the scroll saw and drilling, this might well be the project for you.

PROJECT OVERVIEW

Have a look at the project picture (above), the working drawing (Fig 1-1a) and the template design (Fig 1-1b), and see that we have designed the machine so it can be easily positioned on the edge of a surface. The idea is that the machine can be located on a mantle shelf or the edge of a table in such a way that the weight can fall three or four feet lower than the base of the machine.

Although at first sight this project may look almost too simple to be true, I think it fair to warn you that turning the beam boss with its integral pulley wheel and spindle, plus turning, drilling and fitting out the long, sausage-shaped bob weight, are all procedures that call for a deal of patience and expertise. There are several points along the way that require delicate work if you are to avoid mess-ups. For example, the fit of the spindle needs to be just so—not too loose, not too tight. Also, the bob weight hole has to run straight and true. If the drill bit veers a little off-center, you've got a dowel with a gash in the side—not a pretty sight!

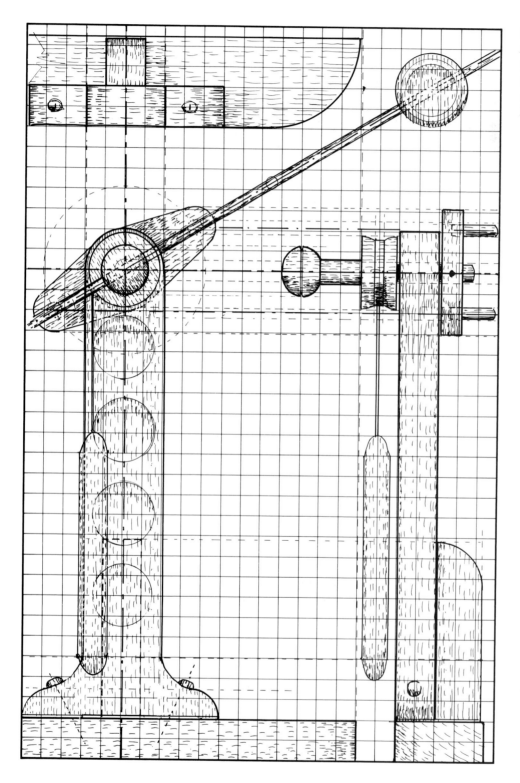

FIGURE 1-1A
At a grid scale of two squares to 1", the machine stands about 13" high and a little over 24" wide across the span of the beam rod.

PROJECT ONE: TEMPLATE DESIGN

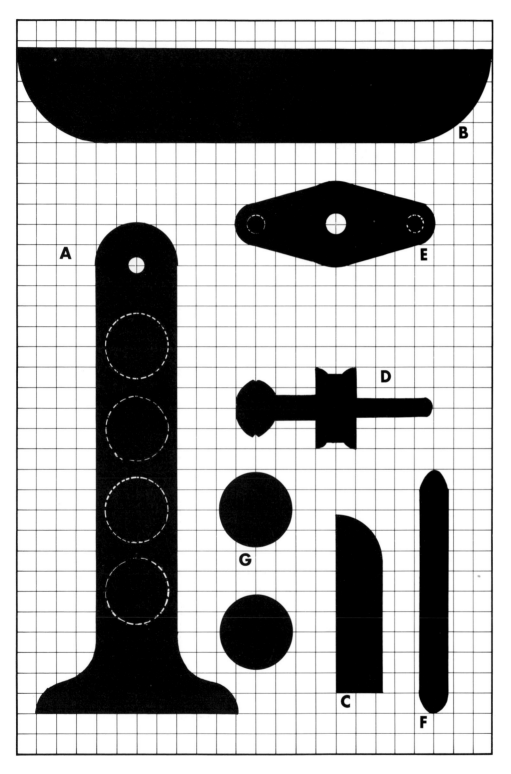

FIGURE 1-1B
The scale is two grid squares to 1".
A *Stand.*
B *Base.*
C *Buttress support.*
D *Boss spindle drum and flywheel cam disks.*
E *Crank handle.*
F *Weight.*
G *Beam weights.*

CUTTING LIST—PROJECT ONE

A	Stand	1 × 5½ × 13½ cherry
B	Base	1 × 2¼ × 12 cherry
C	Buttress support	1 × 1¼ × 4¼ cherry
D	Boss spindle drum and flywheel cam disks	2 × 2 × 12 cherry
E	Crank handle	1 × 2 × 6 cherry
F	Weight	6"—¾" dark wood dowel
G	Beam weights	2 × 2 × 8 cherry
	Beam	24"—¼" dowel
	Handles, fixing pegs	White wood dowel pieces

CHOOSING YOUR WOOD

Although we went for North American cherry for the base, stand, beam weights and crank, a length of off-the-shelf dark wood dowel for the weight, and odds and ends of various white wood dowel for the handles and fixing pegs, this is not to say you can't go for almost any wood that takes your fancy. There are two provisoes: The bob weight is best made from a heavy, dense wood, while the boss spindle needs to be made from a wood that is straight grained and easy to turn. That said—and being mindful that we all ought to be using nature-friendly, sustainable timbers—you could go for a variety like lime, jelutong or perhaps even beech. My overall thinking is that if the wood is easy to work; not too expensive; free from knots, splits, warps and stains; and from a reputable source, it's the right timber for the task.

MAKING THE BASE, BACKBOARD AND CRANK HANDLE

1 Study the working drawing (Fig 1-1a) and template design (Fig 1-1b). Draw the profiles to size and make clear tracings.

2 Set to work carefully cutting out the profiles.

3 Take the two cutouts—the stand and crank—and make sure the position of all the holes is clearly established with punched center points (Fig 1-1b). You need center points for the ½"-diameter spindle bearing at the top of the stand, the four 1½"-diameter blind holes that decorate the front of the stand, the ½" hole at the center of the crank for the spindle, and the two ⅜"-diameter holes at the ends of the crank for the handle dowels.

4 With all the center points clearly fixed, drill them out with the appropriate bit size. Warning: For safety's sake, if the bit size is greater than ½", have the workpiece held with a clamp (Figs 1-2 and 1-3).

TURNING THE BEAM WEIGHTS

1 Having established the end centers by drawing crossed diagonals, mount the wood on the lathe, draw up the tailstock, set the tool rest at the correct height, and generally see to it that all your tools are within reach.

2 Take the large gouge, either square ended or round nosed, and swiftly turn down the 2" × 2"-square section of wood to the largest possible diameter. With the wood roughed out, take the skew chisel and bring the wood to a smooth cylinder.

3 Starting with the two beam disks, or pucks, and working from right to left along the workpiece,

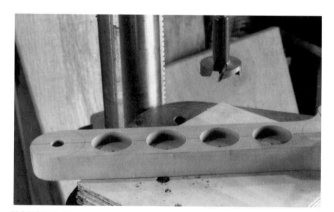

FIGURE 1-2
Clamp the workpiece securely to the worktable, and run the blind holes in to the depth of the head of the Forstner bit.

FIGURE 1-3
Have a piece of waste wood under the workpiece—we use a sheet of plywood—so you can drill right through the workpiece without doing damage to the bit. The waster also ensures that the exit hole is crisp and clean edged.

meaning from the tailstock end, take the dividers and mark all the step-offs that make up the design. Allow about ½" for tailstock waste, 1" for the first disk, ¼" for part-off waste, 1" for the second disk, and then a final small amount for part-off waste.

4 With the two disks carefully marked, take the parting tool and sink the waste areas to a depth of about ½" so that you are left with a core diameter of about ½".

5 Take the skew chisel and use the toe, or point, to swiftly mark in the midlines of each 1"-wide disk. Then flip the tool over, and use the heel to turn away the corners of waste. Aim for a nicely rounded profile. I first cleared the parting waste, then trimmed off the sharp corners, and then rounded each of the shoulders (Figs 1-4 and 1-5) and so on, all the while trying to match up the mirror-image forms.

FIGURE 1-4
To turn off the round shoulder, set the skew chisel flat on the workpiece, slowly twist the tool until the back or heel of the blade begins to bite, and then run in a continuous sweep down and round into the valley.

FIGURE 1-5
Having turned off facing shoulders, take the parting tool and deepen the parting waste to reveal and define the flat face of the disk.

6 Finally, when you have what you consider is a well-matched pair of disk weights, bring them to a smooth finish with the skew chisel and a piece of fine-grade sandpaper, and part off.

TURNING THE INTEGRAL SPINDLE, CORD DRUM AND BOSS

1 Check your wood over for faults and mount it securely on the lathe.

2 Having used the square- or round-nosed gouge to achieve a roughed-out cylinder and the skew chisel to bring the wood to a smooth finish, take your ruler and dividers and mark all the step-offs that make up the design. Working from the tailstock end, allow a small amount for tailstock waste, 2" for the spindle, 1" for the drum, 1" for the length of spindle between the drum and the boss, 1" for the boss itself, and the rest for chuck waste. Mark the 1" drum with a midline.

3 Take the parting tool and lower the waste between the various step-off points to achieve the required core diameter (Fig 1-6). For example, if we take it that you are starting out with a 2"-diameter cylinder, then you need to lower the spindle by ¾" for a ½" core, the drum by about ¹⁄₁₆" for a 1⅞" core, the area of spindle between the boss and the drum by a little over ⅝" for a ⅝" core, and the boss by ⅜" for a 1¼" core (Fig 1-7).

4 With each of the step-offs lowered to the required depth, take the tool of your choice—I like using a skew chisel—and set to work shaping up the various profiles (Fig 1-8). No problem with the boss and the drum and the length of spindle in between—they can more or less be turned to any shape that takes your fancy—but the spindle shaft must be turned down so it is a smooth fit in a ½"-diameter hole. Note: If you can't use a ½" drill

FIGURE 1-6
Take the parting tool and establish the main core diameters.

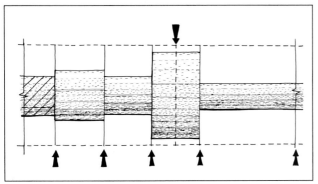

FIGURE 1-7
Lower the step-offs until you reach the core diameters of ½″ for the spindle, 1⅞″ for the drum, about ⅝″ for the length of spindle between the drum and the boss, and 1″ for the boss.

FIGURE 1-8
The partially turned workpiece, showing—from left to right—the boss, length of decorative spindle, drum and spindle shaft. Note that at this stage, we were still undecided as to how we wanted the boss to be finally shaped.

bit, settle for turning your spindle shaft to the nearest available size, say ⅜″ or ⅝″.

5 When you have turned the various profiles to size and shape and rubbed them down to a smooth finish with a scrap of sandpaper, carefully ease the tailstock center out of the way, and have a trial fitting of the spindle through the bearing hole at the top of the stand. Be mindful that it needs to be a good, smooth-running fit (Fig 1-9).

6 To part off, hold and cradle the workpiece in one hand, and carefully nip it off with the toe of the skew chisel (Fig 1-10).

7 Finally, set the rag-muffled spindle in the jaws of the chuck—the rag being used to protect the spindle from crush damage—and sand the part-off point down to a smooth finish.

MAKING AND LOADING THE BOB WEIGHT

1 Before you put tool to wood, have another look at the working drawing (Fig 1-1a) and template design (Fig 1-1b). Note how the weight needs to be long and thin so it can pass between the stand and the spinning beam weights, while at the same time, it must be heavy. Consider how we drilled out a length of ¾″-diameter dowel and loaded it with lengths cut from a 6″ nail.

2 Take your 6″ length of ¾″-diameter dowel and check it over for faults. If it is warped, split, stained, or in any way less than perfect, select another piece.

3 Make a jig that allows you to stand the dowel on end at right angles to the drilling table and hold the dowel securely in place. If you look at the step-by-

FIGURE 1-9
With the workpiece still secure in the jaws of the chuck, draw back the tailstock and have a trial fitting of the spindle shaft through the bearing hole. Be very careful not to jolt the turning off-center.

FIGURE 1-10
When you have achieved what you consider is a good, well-finished turning, use the toe of the skew chisel to part off from the lathe. Be careful that the toe of the chisel doesn't slip between the workpiece and tool rest.

FIGURE 1-11

Secure the dowel so it is perfectly aligned with the drill, and run a ⅛″-diameter hole down to the full depth of the bit. Do this from both ends of the dowel.

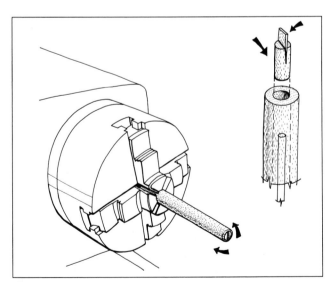

Figure 1-12

(right) Cut a length from a 6″ nail, and push it down into the cavity; aim to finish up with a space of about ½″ at the top of the hole. Plug the hole with a short length of wedged dowel.

(left) When the glue is dry, set the workpiece in the jaws of the chuck, and carefully turn down the end to a round-nosed finish.

step photographs, you will see that we solved the problem by clamping the wood between a couple of heavy, steel V-blocks.

4 Run a ⅜″-diameter hole down through the length of the dowel. Bore the hole down into one end—to the full length of the bit—and then turn the wood over and repeat the procedure for the other end (Fig 1-11).

5 With the holes in place—either right through the dowel or at least a good way into each end—cut one or more lengths from a 6″ nail, and load it to within about ⅜″ of the ends.

6 Push a length of split and glued ⅜″ dowel into the end hole—both ends—tap a shaved wedge into the little stopper, and put it to one side to dry (Fig 1-12 right).

7 One end at a time, secure the loaded dowel in the jaws of the lathe chuck, and use the skew chisel and the graded sandpapers to turn it down to a round-ended shape—like a torpedo (Fig 1-12 left).

8 Finally, cut and finish all the secondary components: the buttress at the back of the stand and all the little pins and pegs.

PUTTING TOGETHER AND FINISHING

1 With all the component parts meticulously cut and worked (Fig 1-13), and with all unglued surfaces lightly oiled, set the stand on the base so it is flush with the front edge and aligned with the center line, and draw in a couple of discreet alignment marks.

2 Clamp the stand lightly to the base, and run ¼″-diameter peg-fixing holes down at an angle—

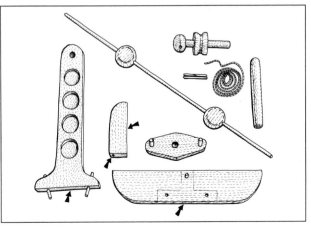

FIGURE 1-13

Note that the areas to be glued, on the base, the underside of the stand, and two sides of the buttress, are not oiled.

through the feet and on into the base. The best procedure is to drill one foot, secure it with a peg, and then repeat the technique for the other side. Be aware that because the feet are short grained, they are relatively fragile. Note: Don't glue the pegs at this trial fitting stage.

3 Take the buttress piece and set it firmly against the back of the stand. When you feel there is good, tight, right-angle coming-together of the three components, fit with a dowel (Fig 1-14).

4 Take the boss spindle and the beam weights and one piece at a time, secure them in an appropriate clamp-and-block jig. Drill out the ¼″-diameter holes for the beam rod. Make sure the holes are aligned at right angles to the run of the grain. Drill two ¹/₁₆″-diameter holes—one into the drum for fixing the cord and the other through the side of the crank and into the spindle (Fig 1-15).

5 When you have fitted the stand to the base and the spindle is sitting comfortably in place at the top of the stand, push fit the ¼″ beam dowel through the boss (Figs 1-16, 1-17 and 1-18), set the weights on the beam, fit the length of fine cord and the weight, and then have a trial run.

PROBLEM SOLVING

■ The whole success of this project hinges on the spindle shaft being a smooth, friction-free fit through the top-of-stand bearing hole. Try waxing the contact surfaces.

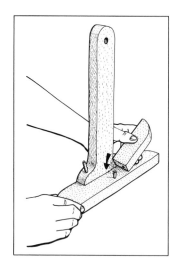

FIGURE 1-14
Fit and fix the stand to the base, and then brace with the buttress.

FIGURE 1-15
Build clamp-and-block jigs for the various difficult-to-hold components that need to be drilled. Minimize the risk of splitting the wood by having the holes set across the run of the grain.

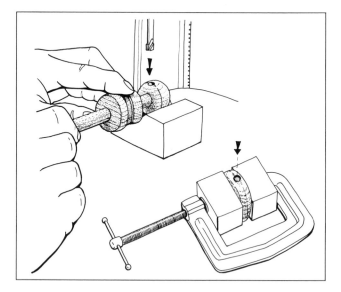

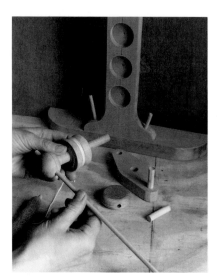

FIGURE 1-16
The beam rod needs to be a tight push fit through the boss hole, while at the same time a loose push fit through the disk weights.

FIGURE 1-17
Pass the shaft through the bearing hole, set the crank on the shaft, and fit and fix with a round toothpick.

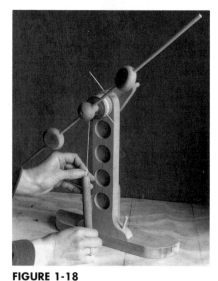

FIGURE 1-18
Fit the weight on the end of the cord, and have a trial run. If need be, reduce the friction by waxing the shaft and all the other moving mating faces.

Harmonic Oscillation Punch Machine

Color photo page 28

PROJECT BACKGROUND

The oscillation punch machine is a gem to make. With its intriguing movement and attractive structure, it is the sort of machine that is just asking to be set into action!

As to the name of this machine, it is not so easy to come up with a clear-cut definition or meaning. OK, no problem with the term *oscillation punch*—it simply describes the up-and-down punch action that is created by the oscillating, or side-to-side, movement of the sector weight—but the term *harmonic* is a bit of a stickler. I reckon it has something to do with symmetrical, harmonic frequency, but I'm not so sure. Have you got any ideas?

The best way to operate this machine is to put your forefinger in the sector weight hole and to flick it rapidly from side to side. If everything is right, the swift side-to-side movement should result in the punch joggling up and down.

PROJECT OVERVIEW

Have a look at the working drawing (Fig 2-1a), the template design (Fig 2-1b) and the various photographs, and you'll see that this project is somewhat complicated in that it is made up of a large number of small moving parts. This is not to say that each component is in itself difficult to cut—far from it—but rather that the sum total of putting all the parts together does require a lot of thinking and a lot of fine adjustment.

Study the working drawing (Fig 2-1a), and consider how the machine is made up of the primary units: a base with a low, glue-fixed backboard, a high, round-topped backboard with a pivot rod location slot and various pivot holes, a plate and spacer to hold the sector, the swinging sector weight itself, the connecting rod, the pivoted crosshead joint and punch, and the bracket.

In action, as the sector weight swings to the side, the connecting rod rises, which in turn lifts the punch in its supporting bracket. And, of course, as the sector comes to rest in the midposition, the punch goes down in its bracket. The best bit about the action, meaning the way the parts move, is the way the loose-fit crosshead joint at the bottom of the connecting rod is kept in place by the pivot pin that passes through the unit and into the backboard slot.

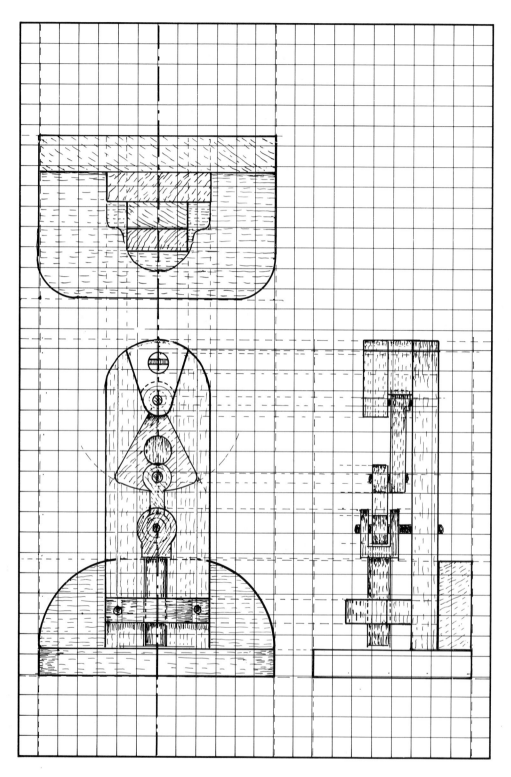

FIGURE 2-1A
At a grid scale of two squares to 1", the machine stands about 8½" high and 6" wide across the span of the base.

PROJECT TWO: TEMPLATE DESIGN

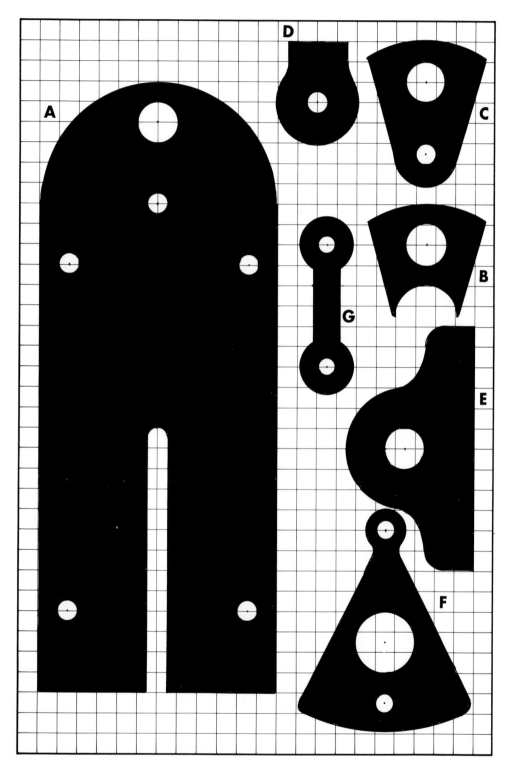

FIGURE 2-1B
The scale is four grid squares to 1". Note that we have only illustrated the difficult-to-visualize components.
A *Tall, round-topped backboard.*
B *Spacer.*
C *Front plate.*
D *Crosshead joint. sides. center.*
E *Bracket.*
F *Sector weight.*
G *Connecting rod.*

CUTTING LIST—PROJECT TWO

A Tall, round-topped   ⅝ × 3 × 7½ oak
   backboard

B Spacer   ⅝ × 1¾ × 2 oak

C Front plate   ⅝ × 1¾ × 2 oak

D Crosshead joint   ¼ × 1½ × 2 oak
   sides

   center   ½ × 1½ × 2 olive

E Bracket   ⅝ × 2 × 3 oak

F Sector weight   ¼ × 2½ × 3 oak

G Connecting rod   ½ × 1 × 2½ olive

   Base   ⅝ × 4 × 6 oak

   Low, horizontal   ⅞ × 2¼ × 6 olive
   backboard

   Pegs and pivots   18″—¼″ dowel

   Wedged dowel and   8″—½″ dowel
   punch rod

CHOOSING YOUR WOOD

We decided to emphasize and draw attention to the various parts by using two strong-grained, fancy woods. We used Spanish olive for the horizontal backboard, the connecting rod, and the middle layer of the laminated crosshead joint and a piece of uncharacteristic English oak for the rest.

MAKING THE BASE AND BACKBOARDS

1 Having carefully studied the working drawing (Fig 2-1a) and template design (Fig 2-1b), take the two 6″-long pieces of wood—the oak at ⅝″-thick and 4″-wide, and the olive at ⅞″-thick and 2¼″-wide—and the 7½″-long 3″-wide board, and use the pencil, ruler, square and compasses to mark all the lines that make up the design.

2 Spend time carefully marking in the position of the center lines, the main peg and pivot holes, and any other guidelines you think will help you on your way.

3 When you are sure all the guidelines are well placed, use the tools of your choice to cut the three boards to shape and size.

4 Peg and glue the low backboard to its base, check with a square, secure with clamps, and put it to one side until the glue is set.

5 Having cut the tall backboard out on the scroll saw, establish the position of the two top holes—the

¼″-diameter pivot hole and the ½″-diameter wedge-peg hole—and drill them on the drill press.

6 Finally, when you have achieved what you think is a good fit and finish of the three boards, set the tall backboard on the base and draw in a couple of alignment marks (Fig 2-2).

MAKING AND FITTING THE SECTOR PLATES

1 Have a good, long look at the working drawing (Fig 2-1a) and photographs, and note how this project is perhaps slightly unusual in that all the small parts are cut out on the scroll saw.

2 When you have a clear understanding of how the parts fit and relate to one another, take the two ⅝″-thick pieces of oak that make up the sector support—the spacer and the front plate—and use the compasses, ruler and soft no. 2 pencil to draw the design on the best-looking piece.

3 With the two pieces of wood clamped securely together, establish the position of the sector pivot hole, and drill with the ¼″ drill bit.

4 Push a length of ¼″ dowel through the pivot hole to hold the two pieces of wood together, and cut the wedgelike shape out on the scroll saw (Fig 2-3).

FIGURE 2-2
Make sure the backboard is set at right angles and aligned with the center line.

5 Have a trial fitting of the two cutouts on the backboard (Fig 2-4). Fix the position of the wedge-peg hole center point, and mark on the spacer plate the area that needs to be cut away.

6 With the pivot pin still in place, use the ½" drill bit to run the wedge-peg hole through the two pieces of wood. Note: Don't forget to back up the workpiece when drilling with a piece of scrap wood to prevent tearout.

7 Having achieved two identical cutouts, take the one that is to be sandwiched between the front plate and the backboard and cut away the waste, the whole ¾"-diameter circle with the ¼"-diameter pivot hole.

8 Cut a piece of ½" dowel to length—so it passes through the sector plate, the spacer and the backboard—saw a slot about ½" down into the end of the dowel, and knife cut a shaving of waste to fit.

9 Align the dowel so the wedge slot runs across the grain, and have a trial fitting just to see if the wedge holds the tenon in place in its hole (Fig 2-5).

CUTTING AND LAMINATING THE CROSSHEAD JOINT

1 Take the three pieces of wood that make up the crosshead joint—the two pieces of oak at about ¼"-thick and the piece of olive at about ½"-thick—and sandwich them together so the olive is the filling and the grain runs vertically up and down. Mark the three layers "top," "middle" and "bottom."

2 Draw the design on the top board, fix the position of the center point, and then tap a pin through the waste area to link all three layers.

3 Run the ¼"-diameter pivot hole through all three layers, and push home a generous length of ¼" dowel (Fig 2-6).

FIGURE 2-3
Saw through both layers so as to achieve two identical cutouts.

FIGURE 2-4
Set the cutouts in place on the backboard, make sure the arrangement is symmetrical, and then draw a couple of registration marks.

FIGURE 2-5
Align the slot so it runs at right angles to the grain, and have a trial fitting of the wedge. If all is correct, a push fit should be enough to hold the tenon firm.

FIGURE 2-6
Saw through the three-layered stack to achieve three identical cutouts. Note how my heavy-handed nail fixing very nearly resulted in a complete mess-up—with a split running along the grain.

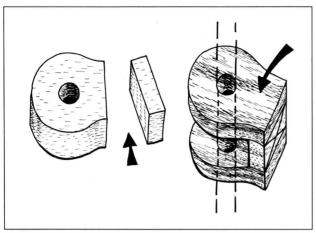

FIGURE 2-7
Cut away the top half of the middle layer so you are left with a ¼″ slice.

4 With all three layers of wood held secure by both the pin and the dowel, fret out the shape on the scroll saw.

5 When you have achieved the cutout and carefully removed the dowel so you have three layers, mark on the middle layer the area that needs to be cut away (Fig 2-7).

6 Cut away the waste, replace the dowel, and then glue and clamp the three layers to make up the unit (Fig 2-8). When the glue is dry, run a ½″-diameter hole

FIGURE 2-8
Smear glue on mating faces, align the holes with the pivot dowel, and then carefully clamp up.

through the base of the component, and have a trial fitting of the punch rod.

MAKING THE BRACKET AND SECTOR

1 Have a look at the working drawing (Fig 2-1a) and template design (Fig 2-1b), and see how the two components—the bracket and the sector—are simple flatwood profiles that are cut out on the scroll saw.

2 Take the ⅝″-thick piece of wood you've set aside for the bracket and use the pencil, ruler and compasses to mark all the lines that make up the design.

3 Establish the position of the punch rod hole, and run it through with the ½″-diameter drill bit. Note: Be mindful that the precise position of the bracket hole, meaning its distance from the backboard, will relate to the finished thicknesses of the sector, the connecting rod and the crosshead joint. If you are at all unsure as to the finished sizes, you can make the bracket at a later stage, or you can allow extra depth to the bracket, and then trim back to fit.

4 When you have double-checked that all is correct, cut out the bracket on the scroll saw.

5 Take the piece of wood for the sector weight—all marked out and measured and with a clear center line—and give it another look-over, just to make sure the three holes are well placed. No problem with the ¾″-diameter finger hole—it can be just about anywhere on the center line—but the two ¼″ pivot holes need careful positioning. The top pivot hole must be at the center of swing, meaning at the center of the ½″-diameter circle of wood, while the connecting rod pivot hole must be centered about ⅜″ up from the bottom of the arc.

6 With all the lines and center points in place, and having carefully checked for accuracy, drill the three holes on the drill press—¼″-diameter for the two pivot holes and ¾″-diameter for the finger hole (Fig 2-9). Lastly, cut out the profile on the scroll saw.

MAKING THE CONNECTING ROD

1 Take the ½″-thick piece of olive you've put aside for the connecting rod and mark it with a center line that runs in the direction of the grain. Mark the line with two center points that are 1½″ apart, and draw in all the lines that make up the design—the two ¾″ circles and the ⅜″ width to the rod.

2 Run the two center points through with a ¼″-diameter drill bit, and then have a trial fitting to link up the sector and the crosshead joint (Fig 2-10). If

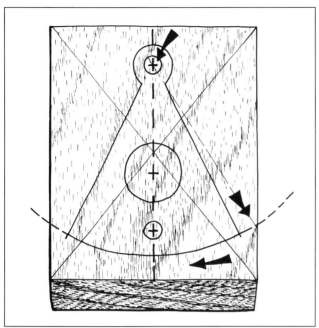

FIGURE 2-9
Avoid weak, short-grained areas by having the design arranged and centered so it is set symmetrically with the run of the grain.

FIGURE 2-10
Have a trial fitting of both the sector weight and the partially worked connecting rod. Adjust the various thicknesses so the movement is smooth and easy.

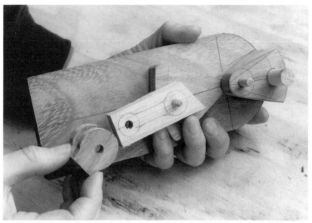

FIGURE 2-11
To minimize friction, adjust the thickness of the wood at the end of the rod and inside the ears of the joint. Use a twist of sandpaper to ensure that the end-of-rod hole is a loose fit on the ¼"-diameter dowel.

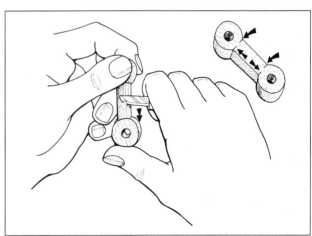

FIGURE 2-12
Use a tight, thumb-braced paring cut to whittle the rod to a round section. Work from the center through to the stop-cut.

need be, reduce the thickness and diameter of the bottom end of the rod so it is a good, loose fit between the ears of the crosshead (Fig 2-11).

3 Having cut the profile out on the scroll saw, take a small, sharp knife and set to work whittling the straight part of the rod to a roundish section. The best technique is to set the circle line in with a stop-cut—on both sides of the wood and at both ends—and then to carefully slice the blade into the stop-cut so the waste falls away. If you work with a careful, thumb-braced paring cut, you won't have any problems with the knife slipping (Fig 2-12).

4 When you have rounded and slightly lowered the round section so the flat faces of the end circles stand slightly in relief, take a scrap of sandpaper and rub down the knife-worked area to a smooth finish.

5 Take the tall, round-topped backboard and mark, drill and cut the various holes and the crosshead pivot runner slot.

PUTTING TOGETHER AND FINISHING

1 When you have completed all the component parts that make up the project (Fig 2-13), then comes the fun of trying to get everything together so it works!

2 When you are happy with the overall finish, glue and peg the low backboard to the base so it's at

FIGURE 2-14

The bracket dowels need to run through all three components: the bracket and the two backboards. Note that—as an afterthought—we drilled a ½"-diameter blind hole in the base for the punch rod.

FIGURE 2-15

Set the connecting rod and joint unit in place on the punch rod, and locate the dowel in the guide slot.

right angles. It's important that everything is square.

3 Set the backboard in place on the base, establish the position of the bracket, and fix the whole works together with a couple of ¼"-diameter dowel pegs (Fig 2-14). Have the pegs running through all three layers of wood. While the ¼"-diameter dowel is at hand, fit the two pegs that limit the swing of the sector weight.

4 Slide the end of the connecting rod into the crosshead joint, push the dowel pivot in place, and check for a smooth, easy fit (Fig 2-15). If need be, reduce the wood—on the rod end, in the rod hole or in the joint—so the movement is smooth running.

5 Push the punch dowel into place in the bottom of the joint, and drill and fit with a round toothpick that runs through the whole width of the unit (Fig 2-16).

6 Take the sector and lower the wood at the back by about ¹⁄₁₆" so the circle of wood around the pivot stands out in relief—like an integral washer. Fit the sector on its pivot, and spend time easing and sanding until it swings with the minimum of friction (Fig 2-17).

7 Use a dowel to link the top end of the connecting rod to the sector (Fig 2-18) so the dowel is a tight fit in the sector hole and a loose, easy fit in the rod end.

8 Push the spacer and plate in place over the sector pivot, and test for fit and function (Fig 2-19). If all is well, you should be able to tickle the sector from side to side in such a way that the punch rod joggles up and down in its bracket.

9 When you are pleased with the fit, finish and function, glue the whole works in place, rub down all the surfaces with a sheet of fine-grade sandpaper, wipe the dust, and give the project a wipe with the teak oil.

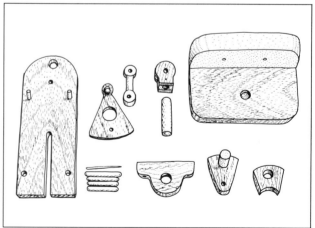

FIGURE 2-13

Check the parts over for flaws and blemishes. Turn a damaged face away so the flaw is hidden from view.

FIGURE 2-16
Set the joint in place on top of the punch rod, and hold the two together with a round toothpick dowel.

FIGURE 2-18
Link the connecting rod and the sector weight with a short length of dowel so the dowel is a tight push fit in the sector and a loose, easy fit in the rod.

PROBLEM SOLVING

■ If you like the idea of this project but want to change the design, it's important you realize that the relationship between the swing of the sector weight and the length of the connecting rod is critical.

■ If you decide to modify the design and are at all unsure about the feasibility of the design, it's best to make a working model.

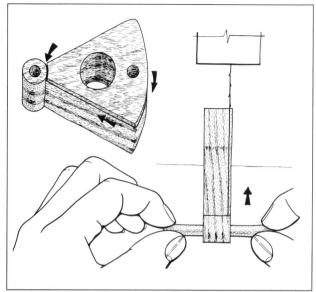

FIGURE 2-17
(top left) Reduce the total thickness of the back face by about ¹⁄₁₆″. Run a guideline around the edge, and run a saw cut down into the face—between the pivot circle and the sector face so the pivot area will be left to act as a washer or distance piece.
(right) If you decide to clear the ¹⁄₁₆″ slice of waste on the band saw, then run a dowel through the pivot hole so you have a safe handhold. Having run a ¹⁄₁₆″ hole through the sector and the dowel pivot and followed through with a round toothpick, set the dowel pivot in place in the backboard hole.

FIGURE 2-19
Set the plate and spacer in place on the sector weight pivot, and adjust for an easy movement.

Cam and Fork Machine

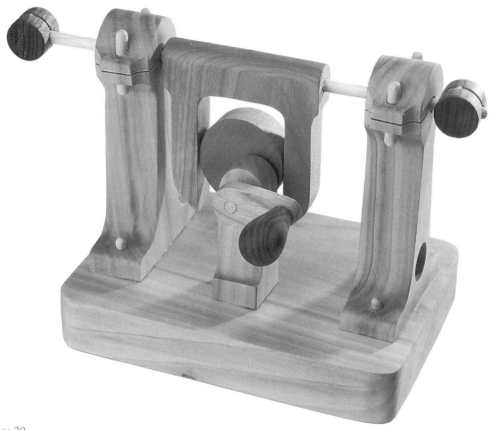

Color photo page 29

PROJECT BACKGROUND

This machine is a joy to make and a joy to watch.

Our dictionary describes a cam as being "a rotating cylinder with an irregular profile attached to a revolving shaft to give a reciprocating motion to a part connected to it." With our machine, the off-center, or eccentrically mounted, disk is the cam, while the fork is the in-contact connection that gives reciprocating motion.

When the crank handle is turned—clockwise or counterclockwise—the cam revolves eccentrically on its fixed bearing, with the effect that the fork and control rod oscillate on the pillar bearings. The fork is fixed on the rod, while the rod is free to slide from side to side through the bearings.

PROJECT OVERVIEW

Have a look at the project picture (above), the working drawing (Fig 3-1a) and the template design (Fig 3-1b),

and note that the disk cam is pin fixed to a shaft in such a way that its movement is off-center. Consider carefully how, when the contained off-center disk cam turns, the fork has no option but to track and follow the cam profile.

Although the design is pretty flexible—inasmuch as there is no reason you can't chop and change various wood thicknesses and dowel sizes to suit your needs—the size of the disk cam, the distance between the fork prongs, and the distance between the side of the fork and the support stanchions are all critical. That said, if you have a notion to change wood sizes, it's best to sort out potential problems by making a cardboard-and-pins prototype.

Prior to cutting the various profiles from your chosen wood, be sure to study the working drawing (Fig 3-1a) and template design (Fig 3-1b), and take note of the direction of the grain.

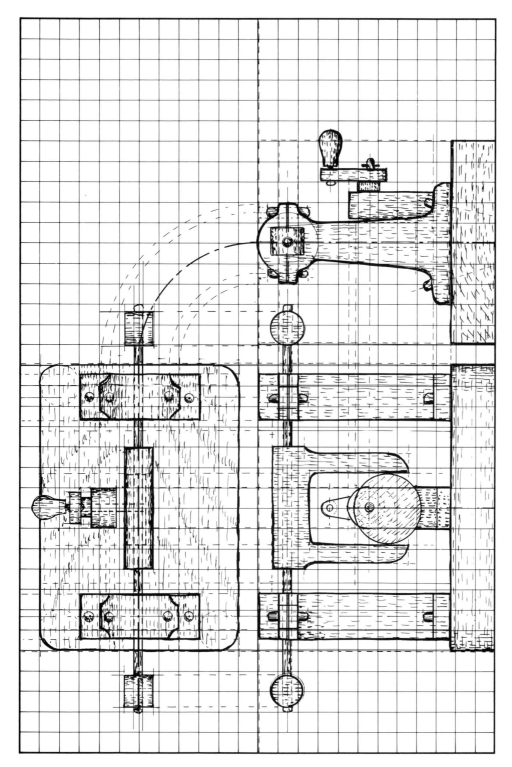

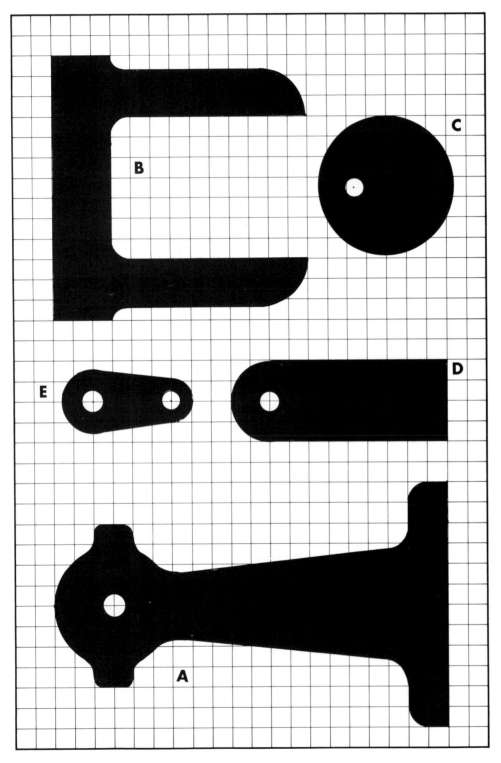

FIGURE 3-1B
The scale is four grid squares to 1".
A *Stanchions or pillars.*
B *Fork.*
C *Disk cam.*
D *Cam post.*
E *Crank.*

CUTTING LIST—PROJECT THREE

A	Stanchions or pillars	1 × 3 × 12 tulip
B	Fork	¾ × 3¼ × 4 cherry
C	Disk cam	⅝ × 2 × 2 cherry
D	Cam post	¾ × 1 × 3
E	Crank	¼ × 1 × 1¾ cherry
	Base	1 × 5½ × 7½ tulip
	Crank handle and end-of-rod pills	1 × 1 × 6 walnut
	Rods	24"—⅜" dowel

CHOOSING YOUR WOOD

This is one of those projects where you might—if you are pressed—reduce wood thickness to suit your stock or your wallet. For example, the base and the stanchions could be a bit thinner—say ¾" instead of 1"—while the fittings could be worked from offcuts.

We chose to use North American cherry for the cam, fork and crank; North American tulip for the base, stanchions, and one or two bits and pieces; and American walnut for the crank handle and rod-end pills.

MAKING THE BASE

1 Take the piece of 1"-thick tulip wood—the piece for the base—and with the grain running along the length, use the pencil, ruler and square to mark it at 7" × 5".

2 Set the compasses/dividers to ½" radius, and scribe out the 1"-diameter circles that make up the design of the corner curves (Fig 3-1a). Use the tools of your choice to cut the wood to shape and size.

3 When you have cut the base to size, use the graded sandpapers to rub down all faces and edges to a smooth finish. Pay particular attention to the top face and edges, and then pencil mark the underside.

MAKING THE STANCHION PILLARS

1 Draw the shape of the stanchions to size on the work-out paper, and then—being mindful that the grain must run from top to toe—use the pencil, ruler and compasses to mark the image on your chosen wood. Repeat the procedure so you have two identical images.

2 Having double-checked from pillar to pillar that the circle center-points, meaning the points that

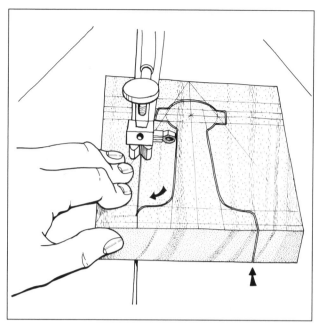

FIGURE 3-2
When using the scroll saw, control the rate of feed so the blade is always presented with the line of next cut. If the cut is ragged, the blade is too slack or the wood is too moist. If the wood is scorched, the blade needs changing or you are working at the wrong pace.

mark the center of the rod hole, are the same distance up from the baseline, use the scroll saw to cut out the two identical forms (Fig 3-2).

3 With the cutout securely clamped flat on the work surface, take the ¼" U-section carving gouge and lower the top-of-stanchion "lugs," or ear-like protrusions, by about ¼". Do this with both lugs on both faces, so when seen in edge-on view, the wood curves down from the face to a thickness of about ½" (Figs 3-3 and 3-1a).

FIGURE 3-3
With the workpiece secured flat on the work surface—with a clamp or up against a bench stop—use the U-section gouge to carve the scooped shape of the side lugs.

FIGURE 3-4
With the workpiece supported on a waster to prevent exit damage, bore out the ¼" bearing hole and the ¾" blind hole. Note: We have removed the clamp for the photograph.

4 When you have carved the lugs to shape so the circle at the top of the stanchion looks to be standing slightly forward, use the pillar drill and the Forstner bits to bore out a ¼"-diameter rod-bearing hole and the decorative ¾"-diameter blind hole. Aim for a blind hole at about ¼"-deep (Fig 3-4).

5 Take your fine-grade sandpaper—and bring all the edges to good order. Aim for edges that are slightly rounded.

6 When the time comes to sink the decorative cut that runs around the top of the stanchion, firmly brace the workpiece against the bench hook, and use the fine-toothed saw to sink the cuts to a depth of about ⅛" (Fig 3-5).

7 Having drilled the two face holes, then comes the tricky task of drilling the lug and foot holes. I say tricky because with both the lug and the foot, the holes need to be run into a curved face. When you come to drill the lug hole—and bearing in mind that the drill bit will try to push the curved surface to one side—first set the workpiece square between a couple of heavy blocks, and then hold it in place with a good clamp. This done, run the ¼"-diameter hole through the thickness of the lug (Fig 3-6).

8 To drill the ¼"-diameter foot hole, set the workpiece on a stack of scrap so the hole is angled in toward center. Use a long, shanked bit so as to avoid contact between the chuck and the top of the pillar (Fig 3-7).

MAKING THE CAM POST

1 Have a look at the working drawing (Fig 3-1a) and template design (Fig 3-1b), and see that the controls, meaning the parts you turn, are made up of a fixed post, crank, crank handle, crank handle pin, or

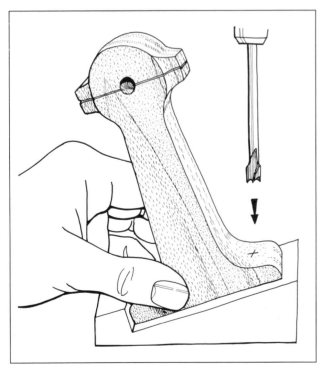

FIGURE 3-7
Make a simple wedge-and-stop jig to help you hold and support the workpiece while the hole is being drilled.

FIGURE 3-5
Firmly butt the workpiece against the bench hook, adjust the angle of cut so the saw runs against the side of the hook, and then sink the cut to a depth of about ⅛".

pivot, washer to distance the crank from the post, disk cam and pivot rod.

2 Mark the size and shape of the post on your chosen wood—we use tulip wood—double-check the dimensions, and then cut out the curved-top front view on the scroll saw.

3 Mark the position of the pivot rod hole, and run it through with the ¼"-diameter drill bit. It's important that the hole and the bottom of the hole are both square and true with the base, so aim to get it right the first time around.

4 Draw in the "feet"—as seen in side view—and then cut them out on the scroll saw (Fig 3-8).

TURNING THE HANDLE, PIVOT PIN AND ROD PILLS

1 Take the length of square section walnut, establish the end center points by drawing crossed diagonals, and set it securely on the lathe.

FIGURE 3-6
Clamp the workpiece between a couple of steel blocks so it is square with the surface and the drill bit, and run the lugs through with the ¼"-diameter bit. Note: If you like woodwork, you can't do better than set yourself up with a good selection of clamps. We have pincer action clamps for small work, toggle clamps for machine hold-downs and so on.

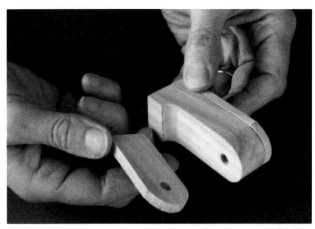

FIGURE 3-8
When you have cut out the little post in front view and drilled the rod hole, draw out the curved-foot, side-view design, and complete the cut on the scroll.

2 Having made sure you and the lathe are in good, safe order, swiftly turn down the piece of walnut to the largest possible diameter.

3 Use the dividers to mark all the step-offs that make up the design. Working from left to right along the turning, allow a small amount for headstock waste—either for the chuck or for parting off—about ¼" for the handle pivot head, ¾" for the pivot, 2" for the handle, 1" for one pill, ¼" for waste, 1" for the other pill, and a small amount for tailstock waste (Fig 3-9a).

4 Having first removed the bulk of the waste, use the round-nosed gouge and the skew chisel to turn down the wood to shape and size. Make repeated checks with the calipers (Fig 3-9b).

5 Turn and sand the string of turnings to a good finish, and carefully part off from the lathe.

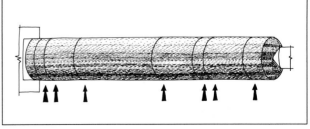

FIGURE 3-9A
Use the dividers to mark the cylinder with all the step-offs that make up the design. Working from left to right along the workpiece, allow ¼" for chuck, ¼" for the mushroom head, ¾" for the pivot shank, 2" for the handle, 1" for the first pill, ¼" for waste, 1" for the second pill, and a final small amount for waste.

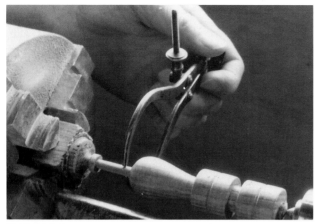

FIGURE 3-9B
Use the calipers to check the diameters against the working drawings. Note: If you are working with a limited number of drill bit sizes, be sure to adjust the width of the pivot shank to suit your chosen bit diameter.

MAKING THE CRANK, HANDLE AND CAM

1 Take a ¼"-thick piece of cherry offcut and use a pencil, ruler and pair of compasses to draw the shape of the crank and the little washer spacer. Plan on the crank being about 1" between centers (Fig 3-1b).

2 With all the lines of the design clearly established, first run ¼"-diameter holes through the crank and the spacer, and then use the scroll saw to cut out the shapes. While the drill is convenient, run a hole into the turned handle to a depth and size to suit your turned mushroom-headed peg.

3 When you make the disk cam, you can either cut it out with a scroll saw or turn it on the lathe, as long as it's 1¾" in diameter, about ¾" thick, and as near as possible to a perfect circle.

4 When you have what you consider is a good disk—nicely sanded to a smooth finish—run it through with a ¼"-diameter shaft hole, and then have a trial fitting (Fig 3-10).

5 If you have followed our directions to the letter, you will need to adjust selected holes or parts of the dowel shaft to achieve a suitable fit. For example, the handle peg needs to be a tight fit in the handle and a loose fit through the crank. Then again, the dowel shaft needs to be a tight fit in the crank and disk cam, while being a loose, easy fit through the little stanchion (Fig 3-11). Play around with the fit until you get it right.

MAKING THE FORKED FOLLOWER

1 If you have a look at the working drawing (Fig 3-1a) and template design (Fig 3-1b), you will see

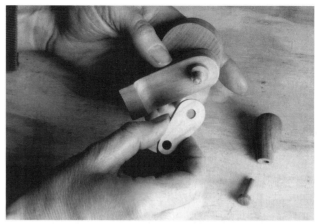

FIGURE 3-10
Have a trial fitting to make sure all the control column parts come together for a smooth-working fit.

FIGURE 3-11
If need be, sand the holes or dowels to achieve an appropriate fit. The little pivot needs to be a loose fit through the shank and a tight push fit in the handle.

that the forked follower, or frame, is cut from ¾"-thick wood, with the grain running from top to bottom and the inside fork width being the same as the diameter of the disk cam.

2 Having drawn the frame on your piece of prepared wood, give it a good checking over just to make sure you haven't made any mess-ups, and then carefully fret out the frame on the scroll saw.

3 If you take it at an easy pace, all the while being ready to pull back if the blade snatches, the cut face will be so smooth it will only require the minimum of sanding.

4 Take the cutout and carefully draw diagonals to establish the position of the through-top rod, or shaft, hole.

FIGURE 3-12
Drilling the rod hole through the top of the forked frame is slightly tricky inasmuch as while the hole needs to run square and true, most drill bits are too short. A good method is to establish the center points for the holes, clamp the workpiece to a square iron block, and then run the holes through from both sides.

5 Hold the workpiece secure with blocks and a clamp so the hole is going to be well placed and true, and run it through with a long, shanked ¼″ bit (Fig 3-12). If your bit isn't long enough, turn the whole works around, and drill it through from the other side.

PUTTING TOGETHER AND FINISHING

1 When you have completed all the component parts that make up the design, then comes the exciting but finger-twisting task of putting everything together. You should have ten primary parts in all: the base, two bearing posts, disk cam post, disk cam, washer, crank, handle, handle pin, two end-of-rod pills, or stops, and a whole heap of dowels cut to size (Fig 3-13).

2 Before you do much else, take the finest-grade sandpaper and rub down all faces, edges and corners to a smooth finish. Give all the surfaces—barring the mating faces that are to be glued—a swift rubdown with a small amount of teak oil.

3 Having cut all the rods and dowels to length, spend time rubbing them down with a scrap of sandpaper so they are an appropriate fit and all the on-view ends are nicely rounded. Have all the ends standing slightly forward by about ¼″-⅜″.

4 When you have generally brought everything to good order, start the fitting by pegging and adjusting the three posts.

FIGURE 3-14
Align the three posts so they are true, and fix with the pegs.

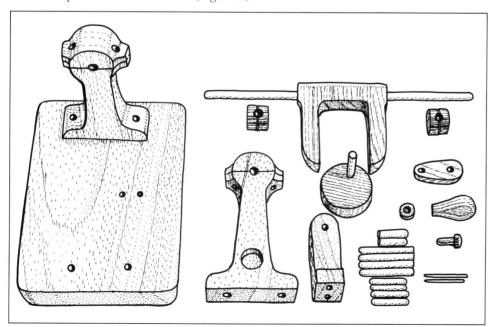

FIGURE 3-13
When you have completed all the component parts that make up the project, check all the measurements against the working drawing and template design, and then sand all the surfaces down to a good, smooth finish.

5 Glue, peg and fit the disk cam, crank and handle, and carefully adjust one with another so they are square and perfectly aligned (Fig 3-14).

6 Slide the forked follower on its rod, and peg or glue. Slip the ends of the rods through the bearings so the fork straddles the disk cam (Fig 3-15).

7 With all the parts variously glued or pegged in place, test for squareness, make sure the machine works, and then put it to one side until the glue is set (Fig 3-16). Finally, give the whole works another rubdown with the teak oil, and then the fun can begin!

PROBLEM SOLVING

■ If you like the idea of this project but want to change the design, no problem, as long as you make sure the cam and fork are compatible.

■ Having made the project, Gill thinks the base and the stanchions would look even better if they were cut from slightly thinner wood. That said, I like the thickness of the wood, but I am not so keen about its color and texture.

■ If you want to make the project but can't get use of a

FIGURE 3-15
Slide the forked frame over the cam, and fit the other post. Note how the top of the frame has been rounded.

lathe, settle for making the crank handle from a shop-bought dowel.

■ As the distance between the side ends of the forked follower and the inside faces of the stands is critical—the machine won't work unless it's right—make sure everything is smooth running before you glue up.

FIGURE 3-16
When you've finally put the whole machine together, spend time making sure all components are square and true to each other.

Circular Movement Machine

Instructions for building this project begin on page 1

Harmonic Oscillation Punch Machine

Instructions for building this project begin on page 9

Cam and Fork Machine

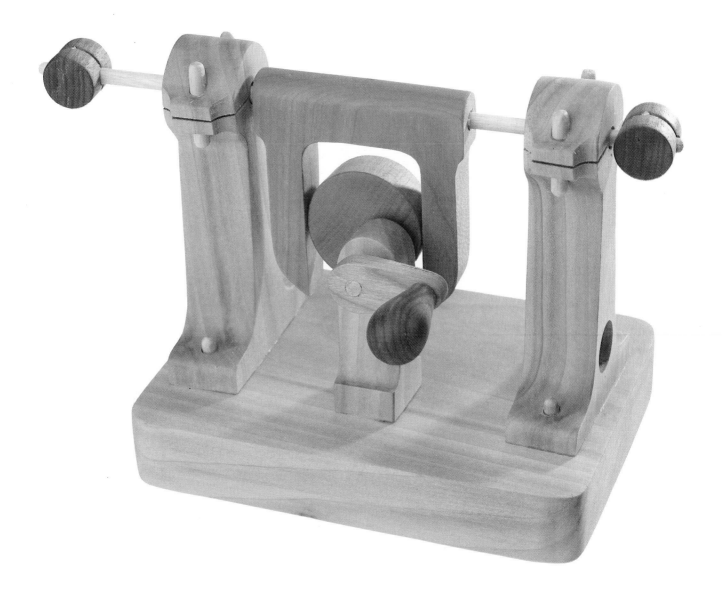

Instructions for building this project begin on page 18

In-the-Round Combustion Engine

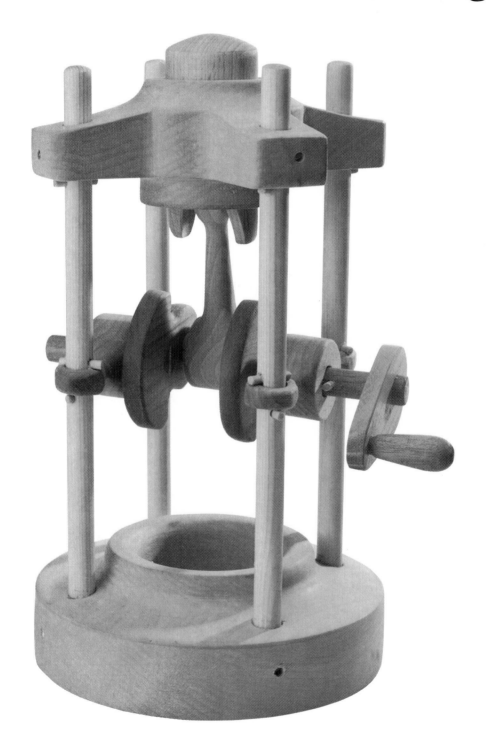

Instructions for building this project begin on page 42

Ward Lock and Key

Instructions for building this project begin on page 52

Reciprocating Engine

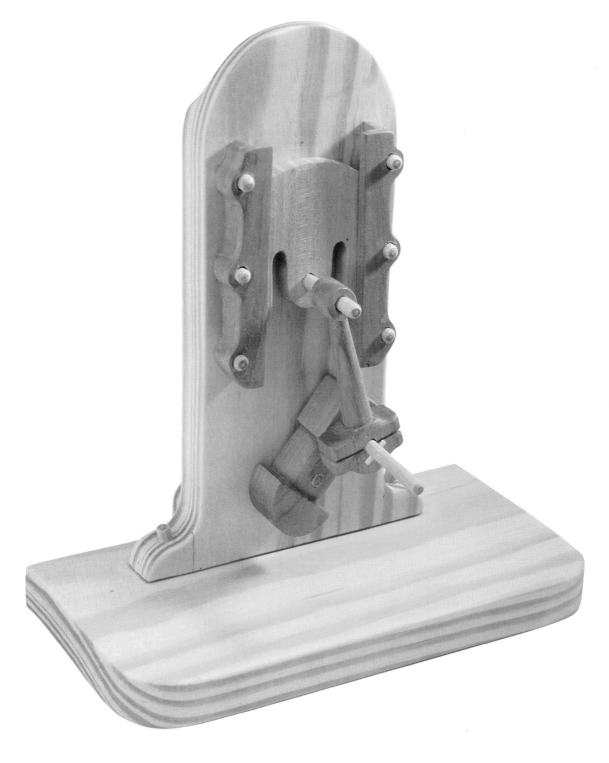

Instructions for building this project begin on page 59

Oil Pumping Rig

Instructions for building this project begin on page 66

Centrifugal Impeller Pump

Instructions for building this project begin on page 73

Sector Wheel Bearing Machine

Instructions for building this project begin on page 81

Flywheel Propeller Machine

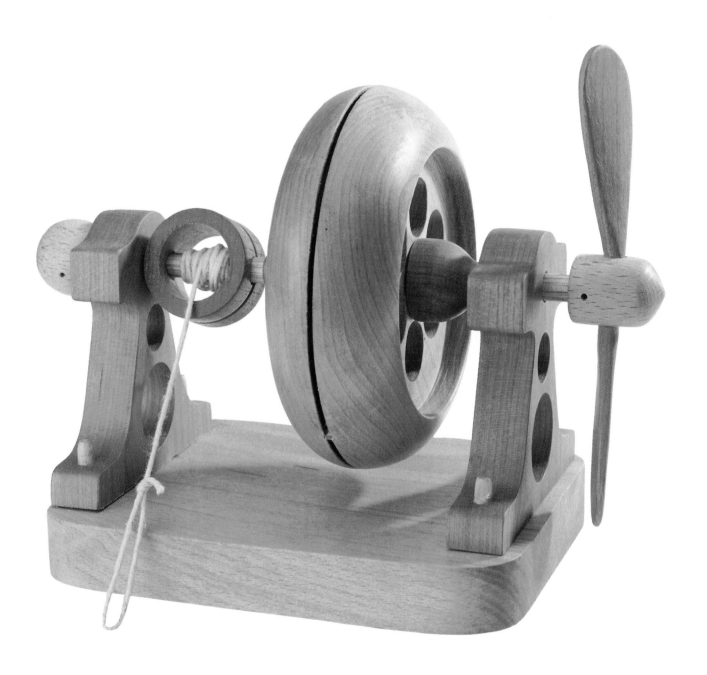

Instructions for building this project begin on page 89

Pyramid Roller-Ball Machine

Instructions for building this project begin on page 98

Rack and Pinion Machine

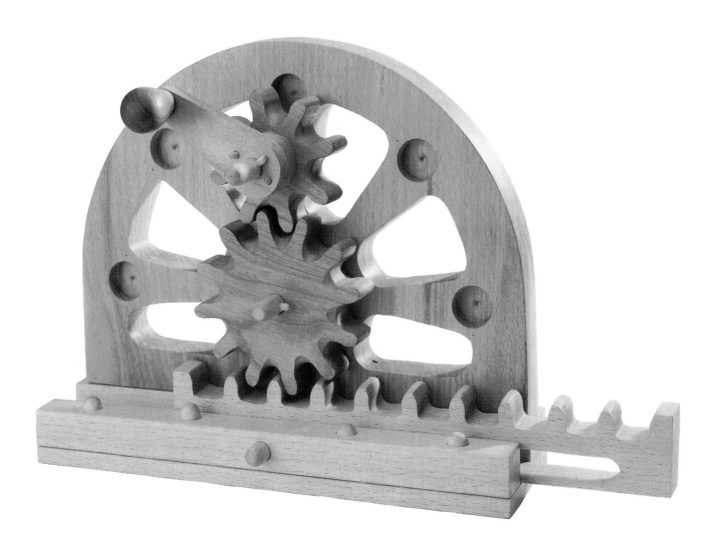

Instructions for building this project begin on page 106

Pendulum Recoil Escapement Machine

Instructions for building this project begin on page 112

Flywheel and Governor Machine

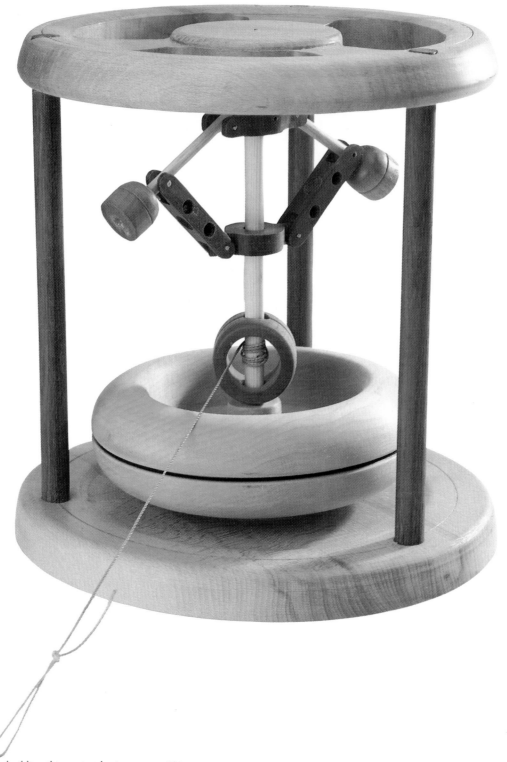

Instructions for building this project begin on page 121

Cam Machine

Instructions for building this project begin on page 130

In-the-Round Combustion Engine

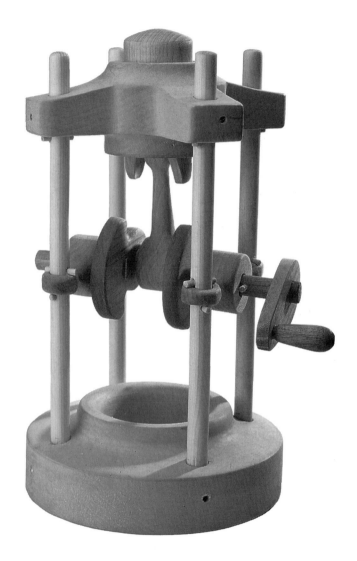

Color photo page 30

PROJECT BACKGROUND

Although the in-the-round combustion machine is in essence much like the reciprocating machine, as shown in project six, it is in many ways all the more exciting in that it can—like a piece of sculpture—be seen and enjoyed from all angles. The turn-handle movement attractively illustrates how the up-and-down operation of a piston is converted, by way of a crank, into rotary motion (above).

PROJECT OVERVIEW

Have a look at the working drawing (Fig 4-1) and the template design (Fig 4-2), and see that at a grid scale of two squares to 1″, the machine stands almost 12″ high and over 6″ wide across the span of the drive shaft. Consider that the greater part of the machine is made up of three beautifully complex turnings: the base, which is drilled and hollow turned; the quatrefoil top, which is both drilled and fretted halfway through the turning stage; and the cylinder, which is turned, drilled and then sawn.

Though the project is challenging, a lot of the tricky procedures relate not so much to your skill level, but to your equipment. Modify the stages to fit your tool kit. OK, so it might take a lot longer, but then, the pleasure is in the doing!

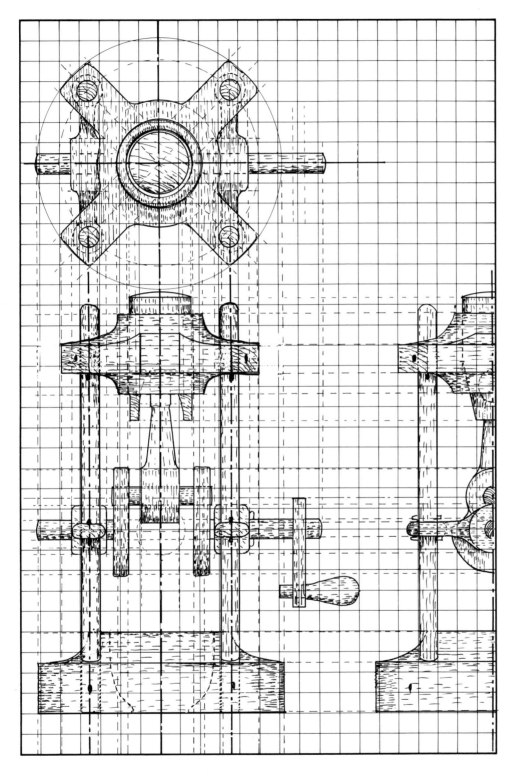

FIGURE 4-1
At a grid scale of two squares to 1", the machine stands almost 12" high and about 6" wide across the diameter of the base.

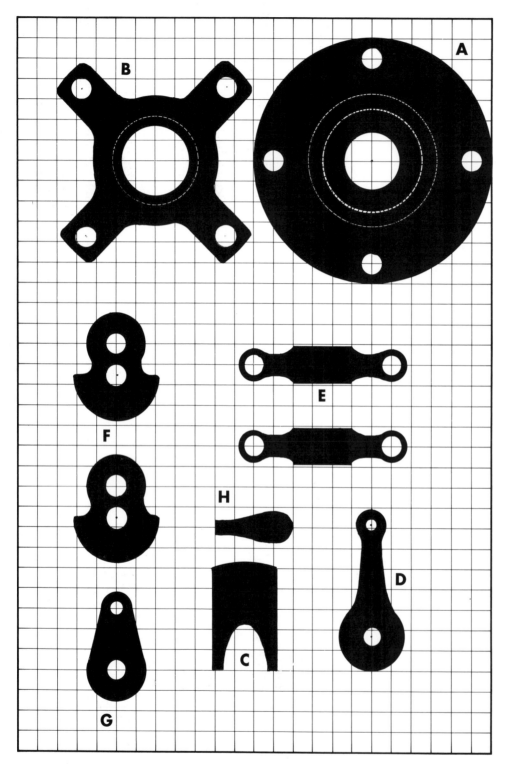

FIGURE 4-2
The scale is two grid squares to 1". Note that we have only shown what we consider are the most difficult-to-visualize views.
A *Base.*
B *Top.*
C *Piston.*
D *Piston rod.*
E *Crankshaft bearings (2).*
F *Crank plates.*
G *Handle crank.*
H *Knob.*

CUTTING LIST—PROJECT FOUR

A	Base	2 × 7 × 7 easy-to-turn lime
B	Top	2 × 7 × 7 easy-to-turn lime
C	Piston	2½ × 2½ × 6 beech
D	Piston rod	1¼ × 1½ × 5 beech
E	Crankshaft bearings (2)	1 × 3½ × 6 cherry
F	Crank plates	⅜ × 3 × 7 cherry
G	Handle crank	⅜ × 1½ × 2¾
H	Knob	2″—¾″ dowel
	Stand rods and shaft	60″—½″ dowel

CHOOSING YOUR WOOD

This is one of those projects where the choice of wood is all important; it's got to be just right. We have chosen European beech for the piston, because it's easy to turn and yet strong across the short grain, and lime for the base and top, because it's both easy to turn and easy to work on the scroll saw.

MAKING THE ENGINE CASE AND BASE

1 Have a good, long look at the working drawing (Fig 4-1) and template design (Fig 4-2), and see that the quatrefoil component at the top of the engine—we call it the engine or piston case—is both turned on the lathe and worked with the saw and drill. Note also the shape of the base.

2 Take one of the 2″-thick slabs of lime and fix the center point by drawing crossed diagonals.

3 Mark the slab with a 6½″-diameter circle. Cut away the waste on the scroll saw or band saw. Screw the resultant disk on the 6″ faceplate using short, fat screws.

4 With the tool rest set over the bed of the lathe, turn down the wood to a smooth 6″-diameter disk and true up the face.

5 Use the dividers to mark the disk with a 2½″-diameter circle, and then turn down the waste so the 2½″ circle stands up as a ½″-high plateau (Fig 4-3).

6 Mount the drill chuck on the tailstock, fit the 1⅝″ Forstner bit, and run a hole through the center of the plateau (Fig 4-4).

7 Mark the lowered area with a couple of guideline circles, one at about ½″ from the edge, for the

FIGURE 4-3
Mount the blank on the lathe, and turn down the edge and profile. See how I use a round-nosed scraper for the inside curve.

postholes, and one about ⅜″ outside the plateau, for the profile line.

8 Having first rubbed down the turning to a smooth finish, take it off the lathe—off the faceplate—and set to work on the turned face of the wood, drawing in all the lines that make up the quatrefoil design. Pencil label the turned face "bottom," fix the position of the four postholes on the guideline circle—at 90° intervals—and establish the shape of the crossarms. Make the arms about 1¼″ wide and all the corners and angles nicely rounded (Figs 4-1 and 4-2 top).

FIGURE 4-4
Bore out the piston hole with a Forstner bit. Advance and retreat with the tailstock so as not to burn or clog the bit.

9 Run the holes through with the ½"-diameter drill bit, and cut the quatrefoil profile out on the scroll saw (Fig 4-4a).

10 When you have completed the cross—all drilled and cut—mount it on the expanding jaws option of the chuck, and set to work turning down what will be the "top" face (Fig 4-5). I used the small, round-nosed gouge and the round-nosed scraper.

11 Rub down the whole works with the fine-grade sandpaper. Do one face of the turning, then turn it over on the chuck and do the other face. If you rub down one face as it points toward the bed of the lathe plus the difficult-to-reach face between the whole piece and the chuck, you will find that the change of direction ensures that all the edges are well rounded.

12 Having achieved a well-turned and finished component, redo the same procedures and turn the base. That is to say, turn down the wood to a 6½" disk and run a 1⅝" borehole through the disk.

13 Turn down the top-of-base profile so the underside rim of the cross is a neat fit in the hole (Fig 4-6).

14 Take the whole works off the lathe—the turning on the faceplate—set the cross component in place so the cross plateau is in the hole, and then use the four holes on the cross to drill four matching holes through the base (Fig 4-7).

15 Finally, remount the base on the lathe and drill, and turn the profile in much the same way as already described. Check your turning against the working drawing (Fig 4-1 bottom).

FIGURE 4-5
With the workpiece held securely on the expanding jaws of the chuck, use a round-nosed tool to turn down what will be the underside of the casing. Go at it nice and easy, all the while being mindful that this is a stage that needs to be worked with extreme care and caution.

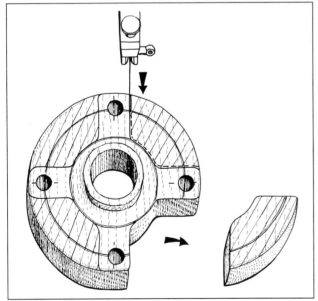

FIGURE 4-4A
Having drawn the quatrefoil profile, use the scroll saw to clear the waste. Have the workpiece flat on the cutting table so the cut faces are at right angles to the working face.

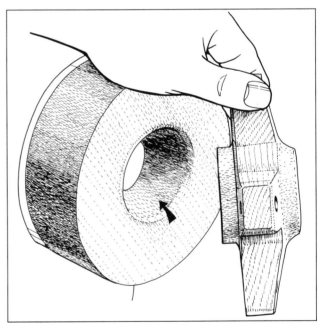

FIGURE 4-6
Turn out the base hole until the neck of the top casing is a nice slide fit.

FIGURE 4-7
With the base still screwed to the faceplate, and using the quatrefoil casing as a pilot guide, bore out the four postholes.

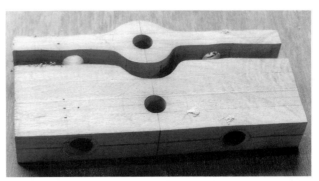

FIGURE 4-8
See how the postholes run through the thickness of the wood.

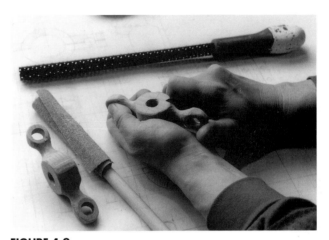

FIGURE 4-9
Use the knife, rasp and sandpaper to whittle the crankshaft bearings to shape. Be careful not to force the blade at the relatively fragile short-grained areas.

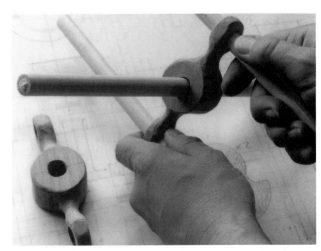

FIGURE 4-10
Have repeated fittings until the components come together for a good fit.

MAKING THE CRANKSHAFT BEARINGS

1 When you have studied the working drawing (Fig 4-1) so you know what you are doing, take the 1"-thick piece of cherry and use the pencil, ruler, square and compasses to mark the design as seen in side view.

2 With all the lines in place, and having first established the exact position of the various holes—both the bearing holes and the postholes—bore the holes out with the ½"-diameter bit. Be careful when you run the postholes down through the 1" thickness of the wood; be sure they are well aligned and true.

3 Take the wood, all marked and drilled, and set to work fretting out the two side-view profiles (Fig 4-8).

4 Mark the plan-view imagery out on the newly revealed cut faces, and then begin shaping and sculpting with the scroll saw, knife and tube rasp (Fig 4-9).

5 Continue whittling, rasping and sanding until you have what you consider are two well-matched forms (Fig 4-10).

MAKING THE CRANK AND CONNECTING ROD

1 Have a look at the working drawing (Fig 4-1), template design (Fig 4-2) and the various photographs, and see that the crank is achieved by having two identical plates and offset dowels.

2 Cut the ⅜"-thick cherry into two crank-sized pieces, draw the imagery out on one of the pieces, and then fix them together with a single pin at one corner. Keep the pin out of the design area.

3 Bore and dowel plug the two $\frac{1}{2}$″-diameter shaft holes right through both pieces of wood, first one hole and then the other. Use lengths of scrap dowel.

4 With the holes in place, begin fretting out the crank shape on the scroll saw. Work at a steady, even pace, all the while feeding the wood into the blade so the line of cut is a little to the waste side of the drawn line (Fig 4-11).

5 Having first drawn the shape of the connecting rod on the 1″-thick cherry and variously fixed the position of the rod holes, fret out the connecting rod profile as drawn (Fig 4-12).

6 Draw the side-view imagery of the rod on the sawn face, mark in the waste, and then slice it off on the saw (Fig 4-13).

7 Use the knife and rasp to shape the connecting rod. Take your small, sharp knife and whittle the straight part of the rod to a roundish section. The best technique is to set the circle lines of the ends in with a stop-cut on both sides of the wood and at both ends and then to carefully slice the blade into the stop-cut so the waste falls away.

8 When you have shaped and lowered the round section so the flat faces of the end circles stand somewhat in relief, take a scrap of sandpaper and generally rub down the whole workpiece to a smooth, slightly round-edged finish.

9 When you have finished fretting and shaping the connecting rod, and drilled out the two holes, go back to the crank plates and wedge the $\frac{1}{2}$″ shaft dowels in place (Fig 4-14). The dowels have to run true, so spend time making sure everything is aligned.

FIGURE 4-12
While you are busy at the scroll saw, you might as well fret out the connecting rod and crank handle.

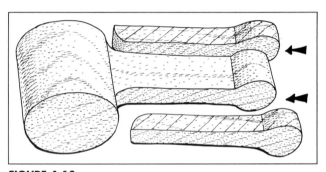

FIGURE 4-13
Slice away the connecting rod waste—as seen in top view.

MAKING THE PISTON

1 Set your chosen square section length of wood on the lathe, and use the large gouge to swiftly turn down the wood to a diameter of $1\frac{3}{4}$″. If all is correct and as described, $1\frac{3}{4}$″ will be slightly larger than the hole that runs through the cross-shaped unit at the top of the engine.

FIGURE 4-11
Fitting the single pin and two dowels at the presaw stage ensures that the two crank plates are identical mirror-image cutouts.

FIGURE 4-14
Slot and wedge the drive shaft stubs into the crank plate. Don't glue at this stage.

FIGURE 4-15
When you think the piston turning is to size, wind back the tailstock and have a trial fitting.

FIGURE 4-17
Use the tailstock drill chuck to bore out the piston waste. Advance cautiously so as not to knock the workpiece off-center.

FIGURE 4-16
Aim for a nice, smooth-sliding fit.

2 This done—and having first set the calipers to the exact diameter of the crosspiece hole—take the skew chisel and turn down the piston so it is an easy-slide fit in the case hole. The best procedure is to carefully draw the tailstock out of the way and then to try the cross casing on for size (Figs 4-15 and 4-16).

3 Fit the tailstock drill chuck on the lathe, and use the 1⅛″-diameter bit to run a hole down into the cylinder (Fig 4-17).

4 Push the piston through the scroll saw—or you might prefer to use a handsaw—and take an angled slice from each side (Figs 4-18 and 4-2).

5 Run a pencil guideline up, down and around the piston, and drill out the ¼″-diameter pinhole—through one side and out the other. It might be a good idea to plug the center of the piston with a length of waste to minimize exit damage.

6 Have a trial fitting of the small end of the connecting rod in the piston (Fig 4-19).

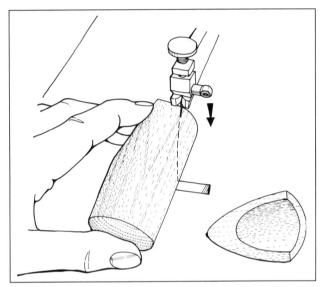
FIGURE 4-18
Slice the sides away from the bottom of the piston pot, and sand them to a smooth finish.

FIGURE 4-19
Have a trial fitting of the connecting rod small end in the piston. The pin needs to be a tight fit in the piston and a loose fit through the small end.

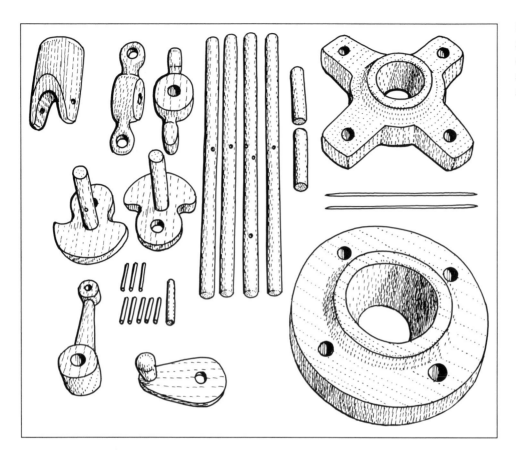

PUTTING TOGETHER AND FINISHING

1 When you have before you all the component parts that make up the project (Fig 4-20), then comes the difficult task of putting the machine together.

2 Start by fitting the small end of the connecting rod in the piston. Aim for a tight fit of the pin through the sides of the piston and a loose fit of the pin through the small end. If need be, rub out selected holes or parts of the pin until everything fits just right (Figs 4-21 and 4-22).

3 When you are happy with the fit of the small end in the piston, take the two crank plates—complete with their lengths of drive shaft dowel—and link them with a short length of dowel that runs through the big end bearing at the end of the connecting rod. Make the rod about 2″ long (Fig 4-23). Don't glue at this stage.

4 One piece at a time, fit the piston in the cross-shaped casing, set the crankshaft bearings in place on the dowel ends (Fig 4-24), and set the pair of bearings on the four support dowels (Fig 4-25). Fit little pegs to hold the various components at the correct height.

5 Continue fitting and sanding and generally easing until the whole machine comes together.

FIGURE 4-21
Pass the short length of crank dowel through the big end, and check for an easy, well-aligned fit.

6 Finally, wipe all nonglued surfaces with the teak oil, glue, clamp, burnish the machine to a dull sheen finish, and . . . hurrah—everything is finished and ready for showing!

PROBLEM SOLVING

■ If you like the idea of this project but want to change the design, be mindful that it's not so easy to redesign a single element in isolation. This being so, we would always advise that you make a prototype.

■ Any time you are ordering wood, it's always a good idea to ask for wood that is well seasoned and dry, but it's all the more important when you are ordering wood for turning.

■ Warning: Fitting the crank plates to the drive shaft stubs is difficult—the sort of task that requires a lot of time, a lot of patience, and not too much glue!

FIGURE 4-22
Fit the crank plates so there is a small space between the plate and the flat face of the big end.

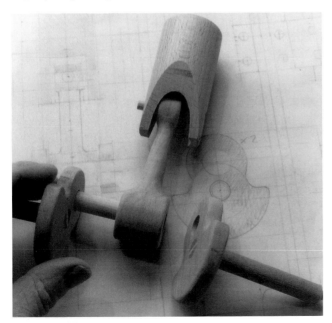

FIGURE 4-23
The crank plates need to have perfect mirror-image alignment.

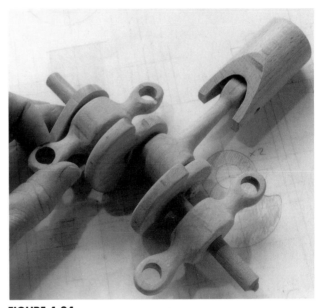

FIGURE 4-24
Fit, check and ease the crankshaft bearings.

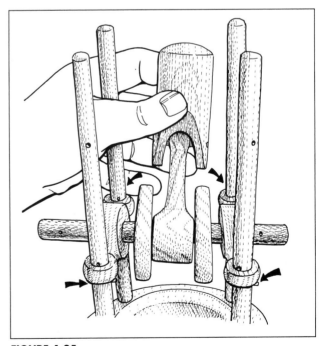

FIGURE 4-25
Set the component parts in place on the posts, and hold them in position with small pegs.

Ward Lock and Key

Color photo page 31

PROJECT BACKGROUND

When I was a kid—I must have been about seven years old—I was absolutely fascinated by locks and keys. As I remember, I spent a good deal of my time collecting keys, mending locks, and generally showing friends and family just how easy it was to escape from a locked room.

Most of us are literally surrounded by locks; we can hardly move without first finding our keys. Yet, few of us know how locks work. The good news is our simple ward-and-tumbler locking machine illustrates all the essentials of the archetypal locking mechanism. There is a key, a ward to block the passage of the wrong key, a sliding latch plate, and a tumbler that holds the latch in place. In action, the shaped key is pivoted past the blocking ward knob, with the effect that in its turning, it lifts the tumbler out of the way and pushes the latch forward (above). So there you go. If you want to know a little more about one of our most common mechanisms, now's your chance.

PROJECT OVERVIEW

Have a look at the working drawing (Fig 5-1) and the template design (Fig 5-2), and see that the locking machine stands about 6″ high with a base slab at 8″ long and 4½″ wide. Note that we have reduced the workings, meaning the number of moving parts, to a minimum in an attempt, as it were, to show the "bones." Of course, most ward locks have a number of springs that bear down on a series of tumblers, but in the context of our machine, we feel that a single heavy tumbler falling down under its own weight is enough to demonstrate the basic principle.

Consider how the cavity has been constructed by setting a fretted front plate against a solid back plate. As for the overall design, we have consciously gone for a solid, easy-to-make, good-to-hold structure. All in all, we have kept the fixings to a minimum so everything is in view.

PROJECT FIVE: WORKING DRAWING

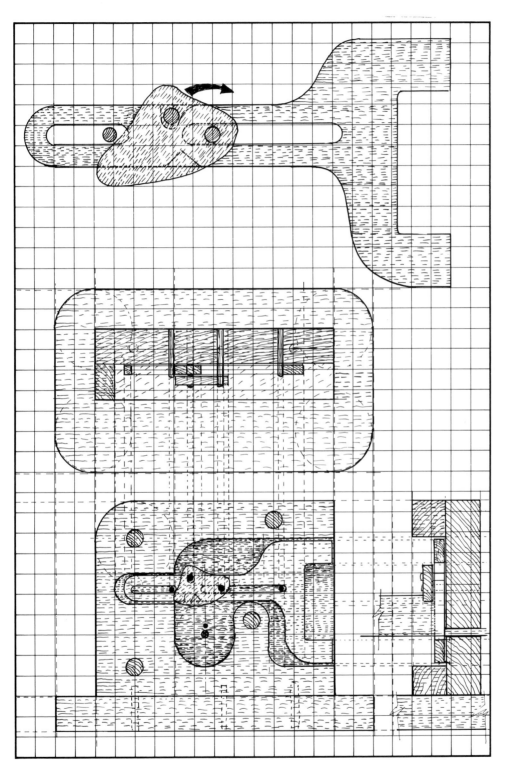

FIGURE 5-1

The finished machine stands about 6" high and about 8" long.

(top) Latch plate and tumbler at a scale of four grid squares to 1".

(bottom) Views and section at a scale of two squares to 1".

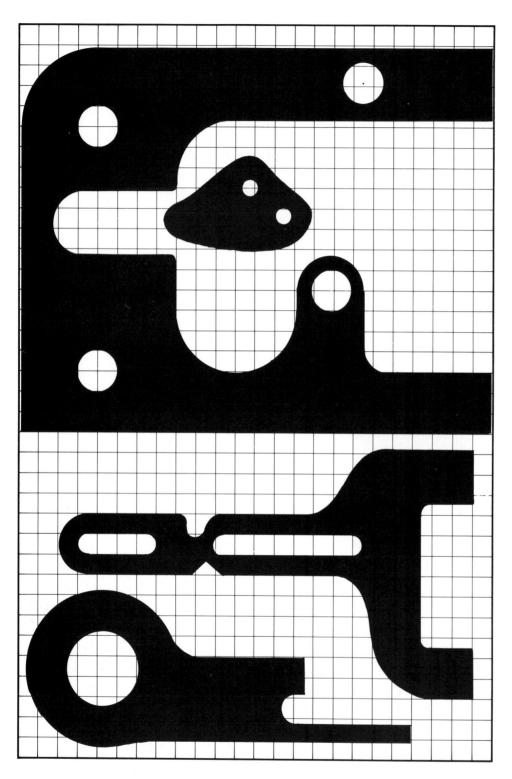

FIGURE 5-2
The scale is four grid squares to 1". With a project of this character—where success might hinge on the width of a saw cut or the placing of a dowel hole—you must take it that these profiles are only broad guides.

CUTTING LIST—PROJECT FIVE

A	Box front	⅞ × 5 × 6 beech
	Box back	⅞ × 5 × 6 beech
B	Tumbler	¼ × 1¼ × 2 maple
C	Latch plate	¼ × 3¼ × 5¼ maple
D	Key	¼ × 2¼ × 5¼ maple
	Base	⅞ × 4½ × 8 beech
	Pivots	¼″ dowel
	Decorative pins	12″—½″ dark wood dowel
	Fixing pins	round toothpicks

CHOOSING YOUR WOOD

As this is a project that is best made from a hard, straight-grained wood, we have gone for beech for the box and base and maple for the moving parts: the key, sliding latch and tumbler.

MAKING THE BOX AND BASE

1 Have a good, long look at the working drawing (Fig 5-1) and template design (Fig 5-2), and see that the main structure is made up of three pieces of wood: a single slab for the base and two glued and pinned slabs for the box.

2 With your workshop in good order, and when you are clear in your own mind as to the procedures, take the three slabs of wood—for the base and the box—and use a pencil, ruler and pair of compasses to mark the design. Mark the base with the corner radius curves and the front box slab with the single corner curve and interior shape that needs to be cut away.

3 Having first pinned the two box slabs together so you have them as if they were a single slab nearly 2″ thick, move to the scroll saw and carefully cut out the single radius curve. While you are working on the machine, cut the four curves that make up the base.

4 Take the two-layer box slab, ease the layers apart, partially withdraw the pins so the points are out of harm's way, and then cut away the central area of waste so you are left with the profile that makes up the front of the box (Fig 5-3).

5 Align and repin the two box slabs, and run the various holes through with drill bits of a size to fit your dowel (Fig 5-4).

6 Finally, take the two slabs that make up the box, set them on the base slab, and mark in the position of the three fixing dowels, meaning the three dowels that fix the box to the base.

MAKING AND FITTING THE LATCH PLATE

1 Take the front-of-box cutout, set it on the ¼″-thick maple—like a template—and use a pencil to transfer the imagery.

2 Having drawn the shape of the sliding latch plate to size and made a good tracing, use the tracing to press transfer the drawn image through to the box shape you've marked on the maple (Fig 5-5).

3 If you have a close-up look at the photograph—in this and many other projects—you will perhaps wonder at there being a great number of differences between our initial prototype drawings, as seen on the tracing paper, and the actual workpiece. The project

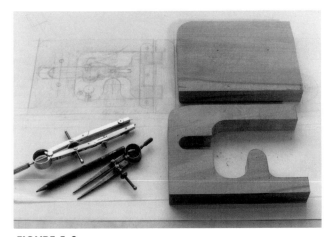

FIGURE 5-3

Having cut the two slabs of wood to the same shape, fret out the front slab to make the latch box cavity.

FIGURE 5-4

Drill out all the primary holes, and have a trial fitting of the box to the base slab.

changes a bit as we work on it. If you have a notion that such and such a shape or way of working is the best way, then that is the best way for you.

4 With the shape of the latch plate clearly marked within the shape of the box, and having made adjustments to allow for easy movement, fix the position of the various holes and pilot piercing within the plate, and run them through with the ¼″ drill bit (Fig 5-5).

5 When you feel all is correct, fret out the latch plate on the scroll saw. Don't bother at this stage to cut the fine details; just go for the main profile.

6 With the plate partially cut out, wipe the edges with a fine-grade sandpaper to remove any rough edges that might get in the way, and have a trial fitting in the lock box (Fig 5-6). The latch plate should slide neatly backward and forward without sticking or racking.

MAKING THE KEY AND TUMBLER MECHANISM

1 When you have completed the basic sliding latch profile and have succeeded in getting it to slide smoothly in the box, then comes the not-so-easy business of fitting the key and tumbler. Start by looking at the working drawing (Fig 5-1) and template design (Fig 5-2), and seeing that the key needs to be cut and worked so the end-of-key profile, or ward, is able to pass over a ward stud that is set in the body of the box.

2 Having first cut out the basic shape of the key blank (Fig 5-7), whittle the stem to a round section so it fits in the keyhole, and shape the leading edge of the key (Fig 5-8) so when it is turned, it catches the notched underside of the latch plate, with the effect that the latch slides forward.

3 The trick to fitting the key is to trim back little by little, stop and have a fitting, trim back some more and so on (Fig 5-9) until the movement is just right.

4 When you have cut the key to a good fit, then comes the frustrating task of fitting the tumbler. If you look at the mechanism (Fig 5-10), you will see that the little, shaped profile of the tumbler has two dowels: the one on the far right, which is the pivot, and the one at top center, which is a peg or knob. In action, the turning key catches and lifts the curved underside of the tumbler, with the effect that it swings up on its pivot. And, of course, as the tumbler rises, the peg is lifted out of the notch on the top edge of the latch, and the turning key goes on to move the latch.

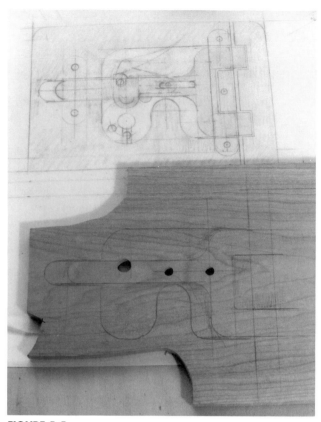

FIGURE 5-5
Having transferred the shape of the box cavity through to the ¼″-thick wood, set to work transferring and modifying the latch profile to ensure a smooth-sliding fit.

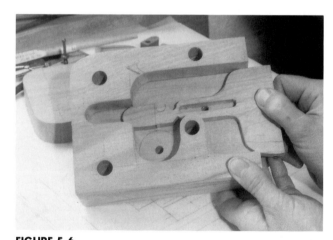

FIGURE 5-6
Fret out the latch plate, and try it out for size. If it's too tight, it won't move, and if it's too loose, it twists and gets stuck—so go at it slowly.

5 Once again, you might well have to cut two or three tumbler plates and play around with the position of the pivot hole and the shape of the underside curve before you get it just right.

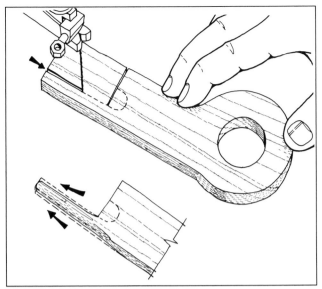

FIGURE 5-7
Cut out the key shape on the drill and scroll saw, and whittle the stalk so it's an easy-to-turn fit in the ¼"-diameter box hole.

PUTTING TOGETHER AND FINISHING

1 When you have achieved a smooth movement of the key, tumbler and latch, take the latch plate back to the drill and the scroll saw and finish cutting the other location slot and the two-pronged bolt profile on the leading edge of the latch (Fig 5-11).

2 Having fretted out all the component parts that make up the project, spread them out (Fig 5-12) and check them over for potential problems.

3 When the whole movement is smooth running, fit the ward knob in the back of the box, and whittle a little bridge ward on the bottom edge of the key so it just clears the knob. The idea is, of course, that only your key will fit into the lock (Fig 5-13).

4 Finally, when you are happy with all the moving parts, fit and glue the dowels and pins that hold the sliding latch in place, glue and peg the two layers that

FIGURE 5-8
Whittle away the leading edge of the key so it fits in the notch on the underside of the latch.

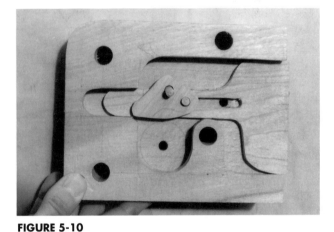

FIGURE 5-10
Shape and fit the tumbler. Eventually, the pivot peg needs to be glued into the tumbler plate and held in place with a round toothpick with the heel end of the pivot running back through the box. The other dowel is no more than a stub that sticks out at the back of the tumbler plate—to rest in the latch notch.

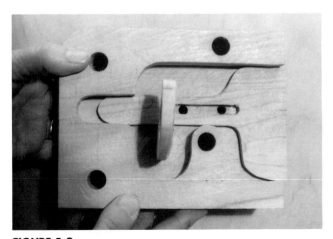

FIGURE 5-9
Continue whittling the leading edge of the key to shape so when it turns, it catches and moves the sliding latch plate.

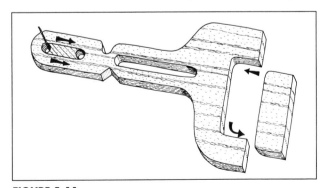

FIGURE 5-11
Having established the position of the slot at the back end of the latch, go back to the scroll saw and finish cutting the profile.

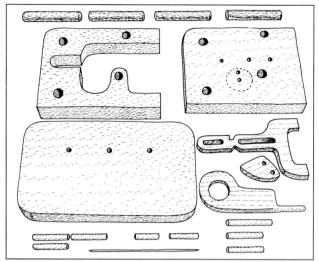

FIGURE 5-12
The component parts—all ready for the final fitting.

make up the box, glue and peg the box to the base and so forth (Fig 5-14). When the glue is completely dry, rub down all surfaces to a smooth finish, wipe the whole works with the teak oil, and the project is finished.

PROBLEM SOLVING
■ If you like the idea of this project you can adapt it to fit other kinds of locks.
■ When we designed this project, we had in mind that we would cut and fit a wooden leaf spring to firmly hold the tumbler on the latch. It's still a good idea; you could use a piece of springy wood, like bamboo.
■ This is one of those projects where you need to hold back with the sanding until the mechanism is up and working. I say this because you might well need to make several keys or several tumblers before you get everything just right.

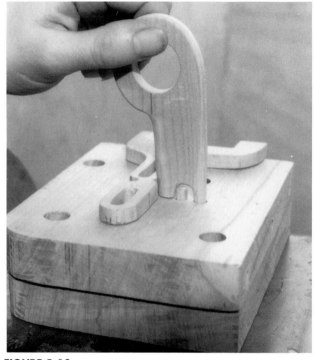

FIGURE 5-13
With the latch being held in place with a couple of temporary dowel pegs, fit the ward stub in the back plate, and whittle the key ward to shape—like a little bridge.

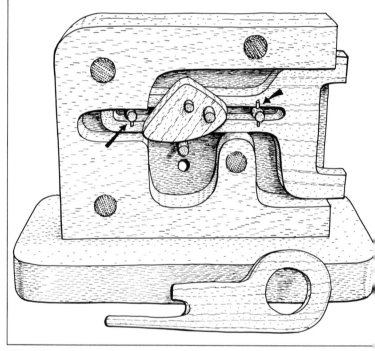

FIGURE 5-14
Finally, glue and dowel the whole works together. Note how the latch is held in place by dowels that are end pinned.

Reciprocating Engine

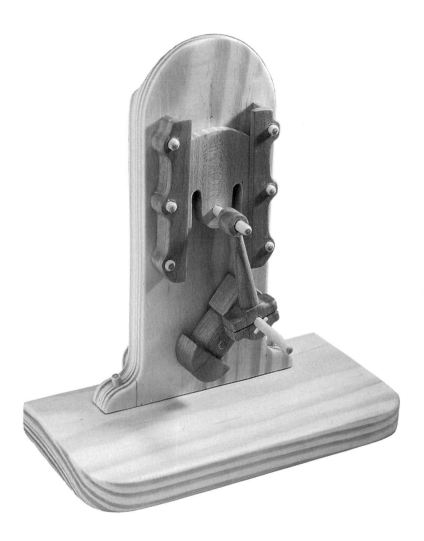

Color photo page 32

PROJECT BACKGROUND

The reciprocating machine beautifully illustrates all the movements that make up the archetypal combustion engine. At the turn of a handle, it's plain to see how the up-and-down movement of a piston is converted, by way of a crank, into rotary motion (above).

If you are looking to make a relatively easy project, this is the one for you.

PROJECT OVERVIEW

Having said the project is easy to make—and it really is—this is not to say you can do it with your eyes closed. Yes, the various cuts are straightforward, and no, you don't need a fancy tool kit, but the cutting and shaping proce-

dures do need to be completed with care. For example, although the fretted side runners can be cut on the fret saw—and this is swift and easy—the various layers that make up the sections of the runners need to be carefully drawn out.

The working action is pretty to watch. As the handle is turned—either clockwise or counterclockwise, it makes no difference—the crank turns on its pivot, with the effect that the piston slides up and down in its runners. But don't forget when you are giving that science fair lecture to mention that the real-life in-car movement is reversed, with the combustion pushing down on the piston and the rotary crank driving the road wheels.

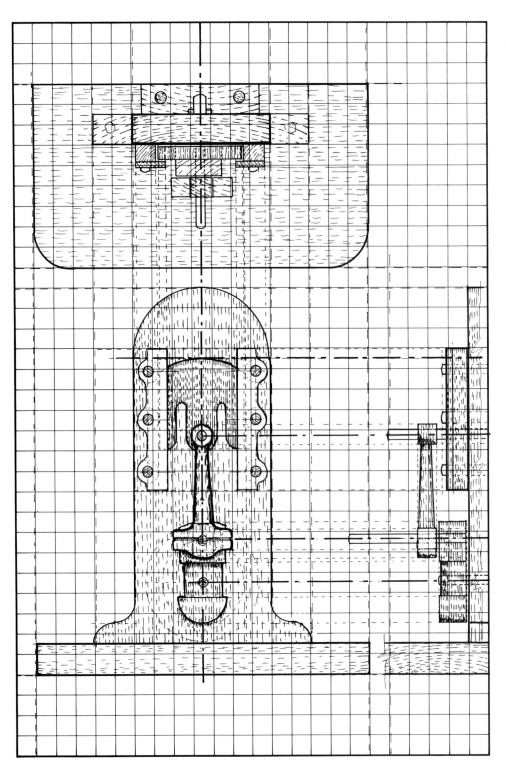

FIGURE 6-1
At a grid scale of two squares to 1", the machine stands about 9" high, 8½" wide across the span of the base and 4½" in depth.

PROJECT SIX: TEMPLATE DESIGN

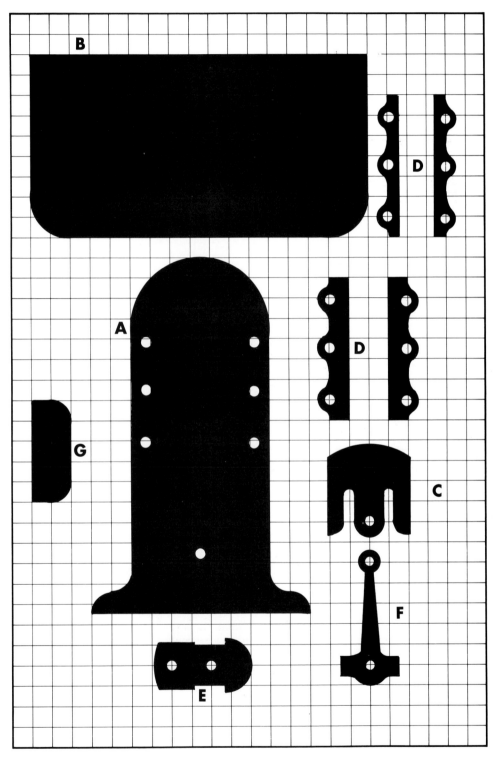

FIGURE 6-2
The scale is two grid squares to 1". Note that as with all the template designs in the book, the profiles are more a diagrammatic guide than actual templates. This being so, it's always a good idea to check out the sizes and the placings of the various fixing and pivot holes before cutting your wood.
A *Backboard.*
B *Base.*
C *Piston.*
D *Slide rails.*
    ³⁄₁₆" thick.
    ³⁄₈" thick.
E *Crank.*
F *Connecting rod.*
G *Buttress.*

CHOOSING YOUR WOOD

If you are anything at all like us—like most woodworkers, in fact—the never-ending question is what to do with the ever-growing pile of offcuts. Yes, it does seem a pity to throw out small pieces of exotic wood left over from large projects, but what to do with them? Well now, no such problems here. This is a great project for using up odds and ends! After searching through our stockpile, we decided to go for straight-grained pine for the base and backboard (it needs to be strong); cherry for the runners, crank and connecting rod; Spanish olive for the piston; and dowels for the various pins and pivots. Note: If you look through the various photographs, you will see that the top, back edge of the backboard is shaped. Don't worry about it. It's not important. It's just a bit left over from another project.

MAKING THE BASE AND BACKBOARD

1 Having carefully studied the working drawing (Fig 6-1) and template design (Fig 6-2), take the two pieces of pine and use the pencil, ruler, square and compasses to mark all the lines that make up the design.

2 Spend time carefully marking in the position of the center lines, the crank pivot hole, and any other guidelines you think are necessary. If you are at all unsure as to what goes where and how, shade in the areas that need to be cut away.

3 When you feel all is correct, meaning all the guidelines are well placed and you and the tools are ready for the task ahead, move to the scroll saw, and set to work cutting out the profiles. Having made sure the blade is well tensioned, run the workpiece into the saw so the blade is always presented with the angle of best cut

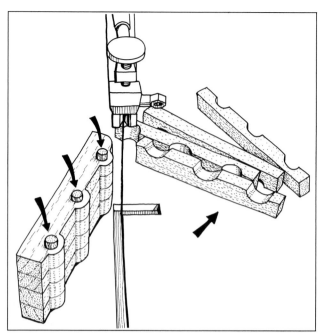

FIGURE 6-3
With the dowels to hold the layers in place, carefully fret out the shape of the runners, or rails. If the blade starts to wander off course, it's a sure sign either the blade is worn or the tension is too slack.

and the line of cut is fractionally to the waste side of the drawn line.

4 Drill and peg the backboard to the base with the pegs run in at a slight angle, check with a square, and generally see to it that everything is square and stable.

MAKING AND FITTING THE SLIDE RAILS

1 Before you do anything else, have another good, long look at the working drawing (Fig 6-1) and the

FIGURE 6-4
Having carefully pencil labeled the layers so they are nicely matched up and you know what goes where and how, slice away the strip of waste from the back layer. It's easy to make a mess-up, so be sure to get it right the first time around.

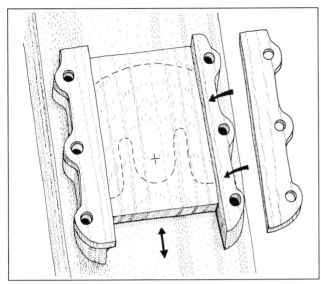

FIGURE 6-4A
The piston needs to be a good fit—not so sloppy it tilts to the side nor so tight there is any friction, just an easy, comfortable fit.

sequence of photographs, and see that the pair of slide rails are achieved by being first sliced into four layers—two for each rail—and then marked out, drilled, fretted to shape and reassembled. Note how the order of work—first drilling and pegging and then fretting—ensures that profiles and holes match up.

2 When you have sliced the slide rail wood into four 4"-long, 1"-wide layers—two at ³⁄₁₆"-thick and two at a little over ³⁄₈"-thick—draw the imagery on one or other of the layers.

3 With the four pieces of wood sanded down and clamped securely together, drill the three dowel

holes through all four thicknesses of wood.

4 Push lengths of ¼" dowel through the holes to hold the four pieces of wood together, and fret out the total three-curve shape on the scroll saw (Fig 6-3).

5 Slice a ¼"-wide strip from the straight edge of both thick layers (Fig 6-4), and have a trial fitting. Label the layers so you know precisely what goes where (Fig 6-4a).

6 Having completed two identical, two-layer rails, carefully set the rails in place on the backboard, and mark in the position of the six peg-fixing holes. While you are at it—if you haven't already done it—mark in the position of the crank pivot hole, run the holes through with the ¼" bit and have another fitting (Fig 6-5).

CUTTING THE PISTON

1 Take your chosen piece of wood and check its thickness by sliding it in the rails. It needs to be an easy, smooth-running fit between the rail and the backboard. If need be, reduce the thickness to fit.

2 Draw the design on the working face of your chosen piece of wood, mark the center line, and fix the position of the pivot. Shade in the area that needs to be cut out.

3 When you have double-checked that everything is well placed—the profile lines and the position of the pivot point—go back to the scroll saw and fret out the shape (Fig 6-6). As always, work at a nice, easy pace, all the while being ready to ease back if the blade starts

FIGURE 6-5
Drill the seven holes, and have a trial fitting of the rails. Aim to have the rail pegs standing slightly proud. Note that the crank peg as shown is no more than a tryout.

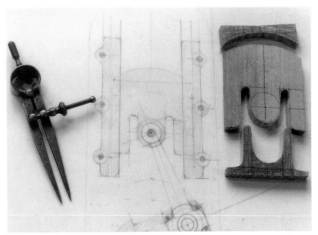

FIGURE 6-6
It's important you go for a straight-grained wood, and equally important you mark the profile so the grain is aligned with the center line. This way of working ensures that there is a minimum of weak, short-grained areas.

to bend or if the line of cut looks to be running away from the drawn line.

4 Finally, take a scrap of fine-grade sandpaper and rub down the edges of the piston cutout to a slightly rounded finish to create a good, sliding fit between the rail tracks and the backboard.

CUTTING AND WHITTLING THE CRANK AND CONNECTING ROD

1 Have a look at the working drawing (Fig 6-1) and template design (Fig 6-2), and consider that the two components—the crank and the connecting rod—are first cut out on the scroll saw and then whittled.

2 One piece at a time, draw the lines of the design, fix the position of the various pivot holes, and fret out the profiles on the scroll saw (Fig 6-7).

3 With all the lines and center points in place, and having carefully checked for accuracy, run the four ¼″-diameter holes through on the drill press.

4 Starting with the connecting rod, take your knife and set to work whittling the cutout to shape. And just in case you are a beginner to whittling, if your knife is sharp, and if you are working with an easy-to-cut piece of wood, you won't have any problems.

5 Having once again studied the working drawing (Fig 6-1), template design (Fig 6-2) and photographs, take your small, sharp knife and start whittling the straight part of the rod to a roundish section. The best technique is to set in the circle lines of the ends with stop-cuts—on both sides of the wood and at both ends—and then to carefully slice the blade into the stop-cut so the waste falls away. If you work with a careful thumb-braced paring cut, you won't have any problems with the knife slipping (Fig 6-8).

6 When you have shaped and lowered the round section so the flat faces of the end circles stand somewhat proud, take a scrap of sandpaper and generally rub down the whole workpiece to a smooth, slightly round-edged finish.

7 Run a V-cut around the big end to achieve the illusion that—just like a metal casting—the form is made up of two parts.

8 When you are pleased with the overall shape and feel of the connecting rod, follow through with more or less the same whittling procedures for the crank. That is to say, set the ends in with stop-cuts, and then

FIGURE 6-7
Run the center line in the direction of the grain, and then have the profile set square and symmetrical with the line. Be sure to double-check the position of the dowel holes.

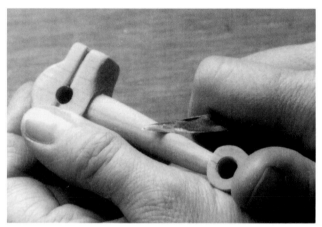

FIGURE 6-8
Work with a careful thumb-braced paring stroke, all the while being ready to brake if the blade slips. Tip: A razor-sharp blade is much safer to use than a blunt blade that needs to be bullied into action.

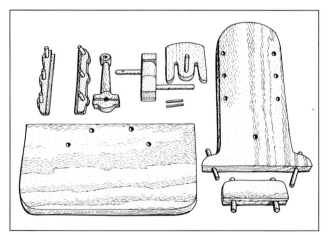

FIGURE 6-9
When you have completed all the component parts that make up the project, spread them out on the work surface, and check them over just to make sure everything is correct.

pare away the central portion so it is half-round in section. Make sure the square, flat end stands slightly higher than the rest of the piece.

PUTTING TOGETHER AND FINISHING

1 When you have completed all the component parts that make up the project (Fig 6-9), then comes the pleasure of putting the machine together.

2 Having rubbed down all faces and edges with a sheet of fine-grade sandpaper, wiped away the dust, and had another trial fitting—just to make sure everything comes together for a good fit—give all nonglued surfaces a swift wipe with the teak oil, and put the whole works to one side to dry.

3 Glue and peg the backboard to the base so it's at right angles, and glue and peg the buttress in place. It's important everything is true, so spend time checking with the ruler and square (Fig 6-10).

4 Glue and peg the rails in place, check that the piston still fits, wipe away any excess glue and clamp up.

5 Glue the three pivot rods in place: the small end rod that stands out from the piston, the rod that runs out from the back of the crank, and the handle or big-end rod that stands out from the front of the crank. Wipe away excess glue, check alignment, and put the rods to one side until the glue is set (Fig 6-11).

6 Finally, slide the crank rod through the backboard, fit the fixing pin, slide the piston down in place between the rails, set the connecting rod on both the crank rod and the piston rod, and . . . the project is finished.

PROBLEM SOLVING

■ If you like the idea of this project but want to change the design, no problem, as long as there is clearance between the bottom of the piston and the rounded end of the crank and between the square end of the crank and the base slab. If in doubt, it's always a good idea to make a working model.
■ When you are ordering your wood, always ask for wood that is well seasoned and dry. I say this because partly seasoned wood is likely to split, warp or shrink and damp wood is difficult to work.
■ Having said the straight-grained pine is suitable for the backboard and the base, this is not to say it is suitable for the small parts that are to be whittled. If you have any doubts as to the suitability of such and such a wood for

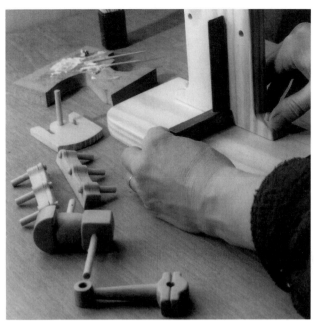

FIGURE 6-10
Having glued, check for squareness before clamping.

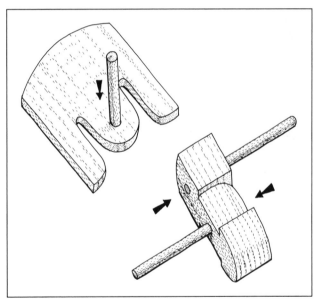

FIGURE 6-11
The movement hinges on the dowel rods being carefully placed so they are square with the working face. Make several checks.
(left) Piston.
(right) Crank.

whittling, it's a good idea to try a sample with your knife.
■ Shop-bought dowel rod is a problem inasmuch as the sizing is variable and unreliable. For example, my so called $\frac{1}{4}$″-diameter dowel is a very loose fit in a $\frac{1}{4}$″ hole, whereas my $\frac{1}{2}$″ dowel is too big for a $\frac{1}{2}$″ hole and a sloppy, loose fit for a $\frac{3}{8}$″. This being so, it's always a good idea to check out your dowel supply at the start of a project, and then modify the project accordingly.

Oil Pumping Rig

Color photo page 33

PROJECT BACKGROUND

We have tried in this project to capture the essential imagery—the tower, or derrick, seesaw beam, crank and nodding donkeylike head. The movement is beautifully direct: When the handle is turned, the crank revolves, with the effect that the beam oscillates and the loose-pivoted donkey head at the end of the beam slowly nods up and down.

PROJECT OVERVIEW

Have a look at the project picture (above), the working drawing (Fig 7-1) and the template design (Fig 7-2), and note that the machine is made up of six primary elements: a base slab, tower, balance beam at the top of the tower, pivot plate that holds the beam, crank and connecting rod. And, of course, there are secondary elements like the donkey head and the various pins and pivots.

This project is ideally suited for the beginner, inasmuch as it can be cut and worked with nothing more complicated than a scroll saw and pillar drill. What else to say, except that this machine is great fun to make and great fun to watch in action.

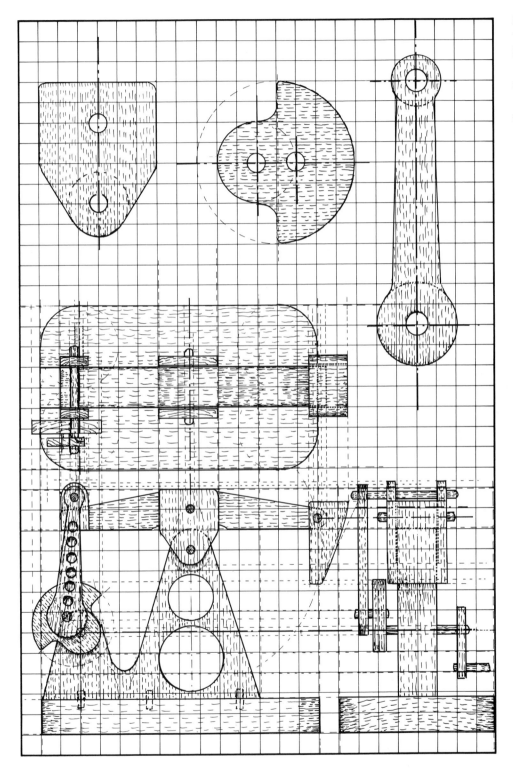

FIGURE 7-1
*The machine stands about 6"
high and 7" long.
(top) The grid scale is four
squares to 1".
(bottom) The grid scale is two
squares to 1".*

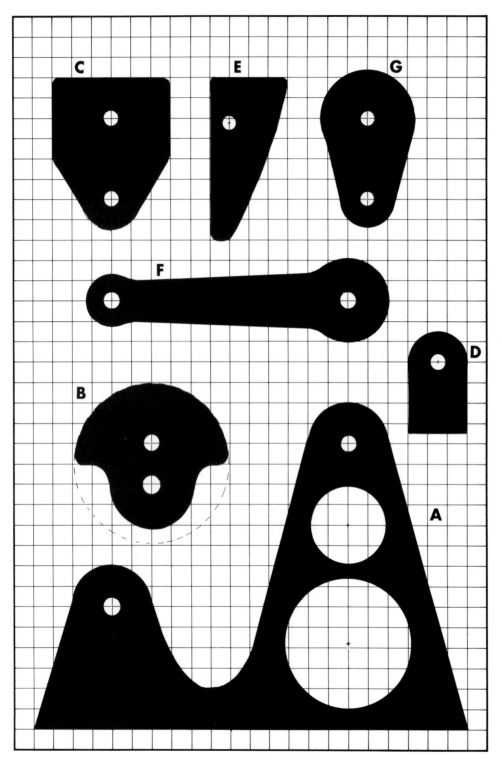

FIGURE 7-2
*The scale is four grid squares
to 1".*
A *Derrick tower.*
B *Crank plate.*
C *Center pivot plates.*
D *End pivot plates.*
E *Donkey head.
    sides.
    center.*
F *Connecting rod.*
G *Handle.*

CUTTING LIST—PROJECT SEVEN

A	Derrick tower	$7/8 \times 6 \times 7$ cedar
B	Crank plate	$2 \times 3/8 \times 2 \times 2$ plum
C	Center pivot plates	$2 - 1/4 \times 1\frac{1}{2} \times 2$ beech
D	End pivot plates	$2 - 1/4 \times 3/4 \times 1\frac{1}{4}$ beech
E	Donkey head	
	sides	$2 - 1/4 \times 1 \times 2$ cedar
	center	$7/8 \times 1 \times 2$ cedar
F	Connecting rod	$1/4 \times 1\frac{1}{4} \times 4$ beech
G	Handle	$1/4 \times 1\frac{1}{4} \times 2$ beech
	Base	$7/8 \times 4 \times 7$ cedar
	Beam	$7/8 \times 1 \times 8$ cedar
	Pivot rods	$1/4''$ dowel
	Fixing pins	round toothpicks

CHOOSING YOUR WOOD

In the context of this easy-to-make project—no wood turning or fancy carving—all that is required of the wood is that it be easy to cut and work. That said, what better wood to use than red cedar? We chose red cedar for the base, derrick, beam, and middle layer of the donkey head; a scrap of English plum for the crank; small offcuts of beech for the various plates and the connecting rod; and shop-bought dowel for the pins and pivots.

MAKING THE BASE, DERRICK AND BEAM

1 Having spent time studying the working drawing (Fig 7-1) and the template design (Fig 7-2), bringing your tools to good order, and generally making sure your chosen wood is in tip-top condition, draw the design to size and make a clear tracing.

2 Take your chosen $7/8''$-thick wood, note how the grain needs to run in relation to the profiles, meaning the shape of the base, beam and derrick, and then carefully transfer the imagery accordingly. The best procedure is to first establish the position of the baseline and the center lines, then fix the position of the center-points for the holes and curves, and then finalize the profiles with the compass and ruler.

3 Having marked the base slab, beam and derrick, and being satisfied with the way the imagery relates to your chosen pieces of wood, move to the scroll saw and set to work cutting out the profiles (Fig 7-3).

4 Having fretted out the three primary profiles, move to the bench drill and set to work sinking the

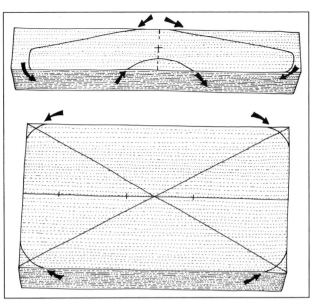

FIGURE 7-3
Although both the base and the beam are simple structures, this is all the more reason they need to be carefully marked. If you decide to redesign such and such a detail, bear in mind that smooth, easy curves are much easier to cut and work than small, tight angles.

various holes that make up the design. Don't worry too much about the two large pierced holes in the derrick (Fig 7-4)—they can be larger or smaller or even placed in a different position; it makes no matter—but do make sure the pivot and fixing holes in the derrick and beam are precisely placed.

5 Finally, having cut out the three primary components and drilled the holes, have a trial

FIGURE 7-4
When you come to sink large diameter holes, the working procedure is to run the bit in for about $1/8''$, then bring it up and out and clear the waste, run the drill in another $1/8''$, clear the waste and so on until the hole has been cut. If you try to force the pace and run the hole through in one great thrust, you risk splitting the wood or doing damage to the drill bit.

FIGURE 7-5
It's always a good idea to stop along the way and try out the component parts for size. This method of working gives you time to assess your progress.

FIGURE 7-6
If you need to cut out a number of multiple parts, meaning identically matched parts, it's a good idea to layer up the wood, drill out any holes, and cut out all the parts at once.

fitting and set them in place one on top of another (Fig 7-5). It's important the derrick stands true to the base and the beam sits square. To this end, spend time sanding and adjusting to a good fit.

MAKING THE PIVOT PLATES AND DONKEY HEAD

1 Before you put tool to wood, cast your eyes over the working drawing (Fig 7-1) and template design (Fig 7-2), and see how various plates and parts come together. Note how the pivot plates at the tail and center of the beam are cut and worked in pairs and pinned and glued at either side of the beam, while the donkey head is made up of three layers and then loose pivoted on the end of the beam.

2 When you have a clear understanding of just how the parts need to be worked, meaning the order of work and the procedures, take the two ¼"-thick pieces of wood that make up the tail and center plates and pin them together with a couple of tacks so you have a two-layer sandwich.

3 Now, having drawn the imagery, fixed the center points, and drilled out the ¼"-diameter center plate pivot hole, tap a length of dowel in the hole to ensure that the holes are identically placed, and run the wood through the scroll saw (Fig 7-6). Repeat the procedure with the tail plates.

4 When you have completed the two sets of plates—all cleanly fretted and drilled—set them in place on

the beam, and have a trial fitting. Pencil label the plates with alignment marks so you know what goes where and how, and decide which of the surfaces are to be glued.

5 To make the donkey head, rerun the layering and cutting procedures as already described, only this time, cut through three layers of wood rather than two.

6 Having achieved the three identical scroll-sawn profiles that make up the donkey head, carefully saw away the waste from the middle layer (Fig 7-7). If you have done it correctly, when you reassemble the three

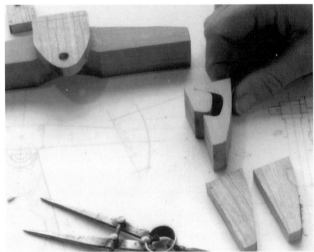

FIGURE 7-7
Having achieved the three identical profiles that make up the donkey head, cut away the waste from the middle layer.

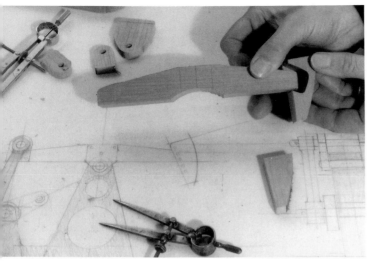

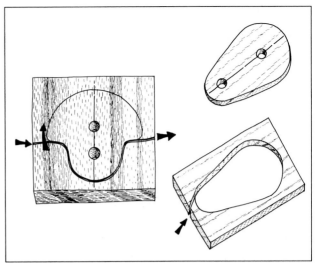

FIGURE 7-8

The head needs to be a loose-rocking fit on the end of the beam. Spend time variously rounding over the end of the beam or cutting the hole bigger.

FIGURE 7-9

The precise shape of the crank plate and the crank aren't too important, as long as the profiles are well placed with the run of the grain and the position of the holes is positively established. To this end, you must double-check the position of the hole center points and see to it that the initial marking relates to the grain.

layers—the thin layers on the outside and the thicker, partially cutaway layer at the center—you should finish up with a little hatlike structure that sits neatly on the end of the beam (Fig 7-8). Check the head for size.

MAKING THE CONNECTING ROD, CRANK PLATE AND HANDLE

1 Have a look at the working drawing (Fig 7-1) and template design (Fig 7-2), and see how the connecting rod needs to be cut and worked. Note that the row of blind holes is no more than a decorative feature.

2 Draw the profiles to size, and transfer them through to your chosen pieces of wood.

3 The crank and handle plates (Fig 7-9) are straightforward: Establish the position of the pivot holes, drill them, and then fret out the profiles on the scroll saw.

4 When you have fretted out the handle plate, check it out for size, and decide how it is going to be placed in relation to the whole structure. For example, if you look at the photograph (Fig 7-10), you will see that in the first instance, we considered having the handle on what came to be the front of the machine.

5 The connecting rod is simple enough to make: All you do is fret out the total shape, run the pivot holes through with the ¼″-diameter bit, and then sink the blind holes at regular step-offs along the center line (Fig 7-11).

FIGURE 7-10

Try the handle plate for size, and make sure there is enough clearance between the swing and the base.

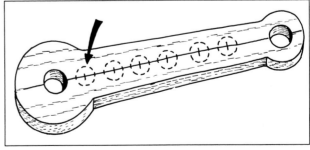

FIGURE 7-11

To mark the connecting rod, draw in the center line, establish the distance between the two pivot points, and decide on the best size of drill bit for the blind holes.

PUTTING TOGETHER AND FINISHING

1 When you have completed all the component parts that make up the design, spread them out on the work surface, and check them for potential problems (Fig 7-12).

2 When you are pleased with all the component parts, take the finest-grade sandpaper and swiftly rub down all the faces, edges and corners. Pay particular attention to bearing faces, meaning surfaces that are going to rub together.

3 Having drilled, pegged, glued and clamped the derrick to the base—and put it to one side so it is out of harm's way—then comes the tricky task of gluing and fitting the donkey head.

4 Being mindful that the head needs to be a loose-pivoted fit on the end of the beam and the beam and middle layer are both cut from the same ⅞″ inch wood, it follows that the head end of the beam will need to be reduced in thickness. The best procedure is to glue and clamp the head, try it on the end of the beam for size (Fig 7-13), and then reduce the beam thickness accordingly.

5 Have a trial placement of the various beam plates, and make sure you are clear in your own mind as to how the parts need to come together.

6 Fit, drill, glue and peg the two pivot plates in place, set the two connecting-rod bearing plates at the tail end of the beam, and glue and clamp them in place.

FIGURE 7-13
Having glued and clamped the donkey head, try it on for size, and reduce the width of the beam end for a loose fit.

7 When you are happy with the placement of the various plates, set the donkey head on the beam, and fit with a pivot rod. Make sure the head is a loose-nodding fit (Fig 7-14).

8 Finally, glue the two rods in place in the crank plate, set all the pins in place, and have a trial run to test out the movement.

PROBLEM SOLVING

■ As always, much will depend on your tool kit. If you can't get use of large drill bit sizes or you have to make your own dowels or whatever, you will of course have to modify the techniques accordingly.

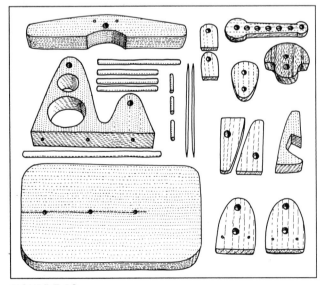

FIGURE 7-12
Set out all the component parts—all drilled and with most of the raw edges sanded back—and check them over for potential problems.

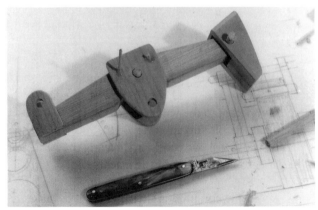

FIGURE 7-14
Drill and pivot the donkey head so it is a loose-nodding fit. If you've got it right, the peg should be a tight fit through the beam and a loose fit through the sides of the head.

Centrifugal Impeller Pump

Color photo page 34

PROJECT BACKGROUND

The poor, old, impeller pump is one of those clever little bits of unsung machinery that's been around for such a long time that we either take it for granted or simply don't know it's there! Centrifugal impeller pumps are used primarily to move liquid along pipes. And they aren't too particular about the liquid: water, oil, petroleum, beer—it's all the same to them.

The classic centrifugal impeller pump consists of a wheel enclosed within a hollow chamber or reservoir, with the wheel having sliding gates and the chamber having slots or holes. In action, when the wheel spins around, the gates fly outward, with the effect that the liquid within the box is suddenly caught up in an enclosed space that

is getting smaller. And, of course, when the body of fast-moving liquid passes one of the slots or holes, it is forced out under pressure.

With our pump, when the crank handle is turned, the centrifugal force causes the little gates to slide out of their slots and follow the casing profile (above).

PROJECT OVERVIEW

Have a look at the working drawing (Fig 8-1) and the template design (Fig 8-2), and see that in essence, the machine is made up of four primary elements: a fretted base slab, cradle and collar, turned tube, or chamber, that sits in the cradle, and turned shaft with integral vanes, or gates, that pivot within the chamber.

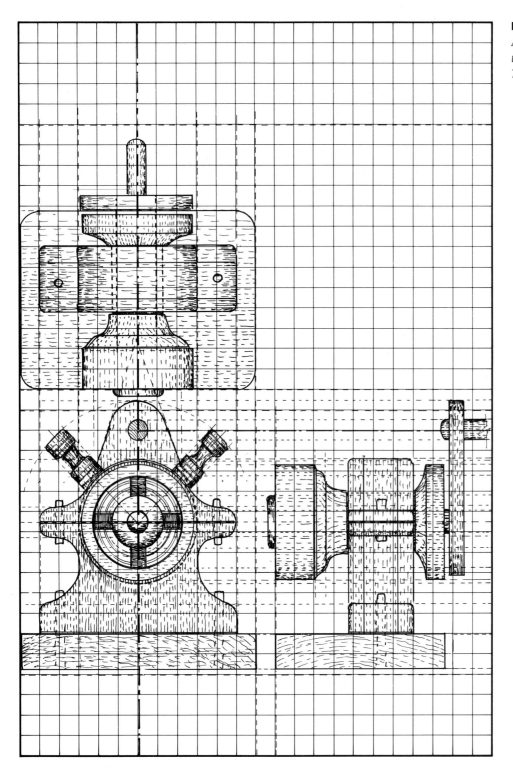

FIGURE 8-1
At a grid scale of two squares to 1", the machine stands about 7" high with a slab at 6" long.

You'll enjoy complete plans and clear instructions for a variety of enjoyable projects like:

- Colonial Wall Cupboard
- Porch Swing
- Collector's Coffee Table
- CD Rack
- French Provincial Corner Cupboard
- Cigar Humidor
- Kids Chairs & Table
- Turned Candlesticks
- Mission Style Table
- Country Farm Dining Table

- Master Craftsman Buffet
- Wooden Drum
- Sportsman's Desk
- Toy Cars
- Traveling Lawn Chair
- Plant Stand
- Flap-top Table
- Lawn-Lantern Bird Feeder
- Cedar-lined Hope Chest and more!

PROJECT EIGHT: TEMPLATE DESIGN

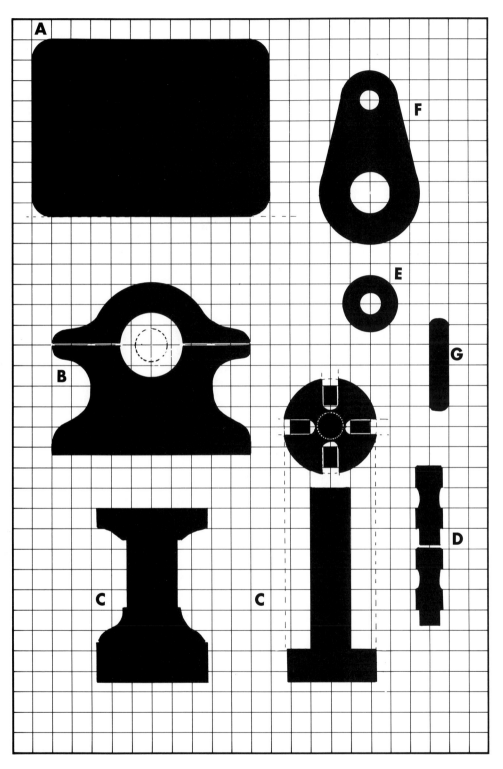

FIGURE 8-2
The scale is two grid squares to 1".
A *Base slab.*
B *Cradle.*
  sides.
  center.
C *Main turnings.*
  chamber.
  shaft.
D *Pipes.*
E *Boss ring.*
F *Crank plate.*
G *Crank handle.*

CUTTING LIST—PROJECT EIGHT

A	Base slab	7/8 × 4½ × 7 beech
B	Cradle	
	sides	2—½ × 6 × 6 plum
	center	7/8 × 6 × 6 beech
C	Main turnings	4 × 4 × 20 sycamore
	chamber	
	shaft	
D	Pipes	1 × 1 beech
E	Boss ring	½ × 1¾ × 1¾ plum
F	Crank plate	3/8 × 2½ × 4¼ plum
G	Crank handle	2¼"—½" white dowel

MAKING THE BASE, CRADLE AND CRANK HANDLE

1 When you have studied the working drawing (Fig 8-1), template design (Fig 8-2), and the various hands-on illustrations, and when you have gathered your wood and brought your tools to order, draw the design to size, and make a tracing.

2 Take your chosen pieces of wood—the piece for the slab and the piece for the crank plate—and use the square, ruler and compasses to mark the profiles.

3 Having marked the slab and crank handle, take the three layers that make up the cradle, and sandwich them together so that you have a total slab thickness of about 1¾".

4 Take the pencil, ruler and compasses and mark the shape of the cradle on the topmost layer of the sandwich. Make sure you arrange the profile so the grain runs through the cradle from the top down to baseline.

5 With the design carefully drawn out, tap three or four thin pins through the sandwich—down through the area of waste that is to be cut away—to ensure the three layers stay put.

6 When you are happy with the layout, use the scroll saw to cut out the profile.

7 Continue feeding the wood into the saw, slowly maneuvering around the curves, cutting out the circle of waste and so on until the profile is cut out (Fig 8-3).

8 Take the crank plate, drill the holes through on the drill press, and then fret out the shape on the scroll saw (Fig 8-4).

FIGURE 8-3
Secure the sandwich with pins and fret out the form on the scroll saw. Be careful at the end of the cut—when the layers are no longer pinned—that the layers don't slide out of kilter.

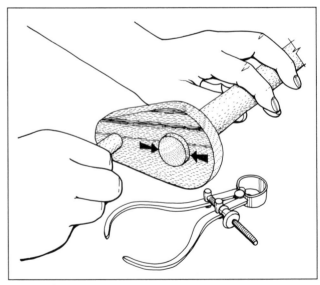

FIGURE 8-4
Check the crank handle for shape and size—I use a length of dowel—and take an accurate caliper reading of the shaft hole.

9 Finally, sand the parts to a good, smooth, round-edged finish.

TURNING THE CHAMBER AND SHAFT

1 Before you put tool to wood, have a look at the working drawing (Fig 8-1), the template design (Fig 8-2) and various hands-on photographs, and see that the main body of the pump is made up of two components: a hollow chamber and shaft. Note the way the outside of the shaft is spigoted and the inside of the chamber is stepped so the two come together for a smooth-turning, sliding fit. Having noted that we've turned the two component parts from a single length of wood, this is not to say you can't go for two separate turnings.

2 When you are clear on the order of work and the procedures, take your 4″×4″-square section of easy-to-turn wood—we use sycamore—and establish the end center points by drawing crossed diagonals.

3 Turn down the wood to a round section of about 3″, then take the ruler and dividers and mark along the cylinder all the step-offs that make up the design. Working from right to left, that is, from the tailstock end, allow a small amount for tailstock waste, ½″ for the back end of the chamber, ⅜″ for the first cove, about 1⅞″ for the neck, ⅜″ for the next cove, ⅜″ for the bead, 1″ for what will be the front band of the chamber, about ⅜″ for waste, ⅞″ for what will be the spigoted end of the drive shaft, meaning the bit with the sliding gates, 4″ for the length of the shaft, and the remainder for headstock waste (Fig 8-5).

4 With all the primary step-off guidelines in place, use the parting tool and round-nosed gouge to sink the main blocks of waste (Fig 8-6). Aim to finish up with a chamber neck at about 1½″ in diameter so it's a nice, comfortable fit in the cradle collar. Sink the between-component waste so you are left with a central core at about 1″.

5 With the chamber profile crisply roughed out, take the tool of your choice—we use a round-nosed scraper—and carefully turn the decorative coves and beading to shape (Fig 8-7). As to the precise shape of the coves and beads, look to the template design (Fig 8-2) and see that they are really open to your own interpretation.

6 When you have achieved what you consider is a good chamber profile, follow through the sizing and roughing out procedures as already described, and turn down the shaft and spigot to shape. The spigot needs

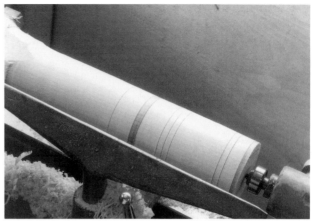
FIGURE 8-5
Mark all the step-offs that make up the design, and shade in the bands of part-off waste so as to avoid mess-ups. If you think it helps, pencil label the other areas.

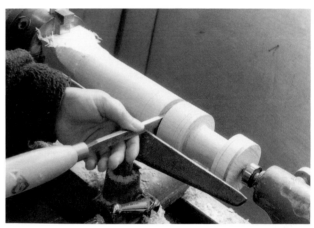
FIGURE 8-6
Use the parting tool to swiftly sink the large areas of waste. Be wary when you are sinking the narrow trench of waste that the tool doesn't get stuck and bind. To this end, best cut the trench slightly wider than your tool.

FIGURE 8-7
Use a round-nosed gouge or scraper to turn the rounded cove curves to shape. Be watchful that the tool doesn't snag and jump.

FIGURE 8-8

Having brought the turning to a good finish, fit the 1"-diameter bit in the tailstock drill chuck and run the shaft hole into a depth of a couple of inches. Be careful when you enter and exit that you don't knock the workpiece off-center.

to fit the hole made by a 2⅛"-diameter bit, while the shaft needs to be a sliding fit in a 1"-diameter hole.

7 When you have completed both turnings—the chamber and shaft—sink the 1"-diameter hole in the end of the chamber to a depth of about 2", and part them off from the lathe (Fig 8-8).

8 Take the shaft and mount it on the lathe so the stem of the shaft is held secure in the jaws of the chuck and the spigot end is centered and pivoted on the live center at the tailstock. This done, use the parting tool and the skew chisel to turn the boss and decorative rings and to generally clean up (Fig 8-9).

9 When you are pleased with the shaft, remove it from the lathe, and mount the chamber with the back end of the chamber held in the chuck—the end with the blind hole—and the front end pivoted on the live tailstock center.

10 Face up the front end of the chamber, fit the drill chuck in the tailstock, and set to work boring out the two holes—the large one at 2⅛" diameter and the other end of the 1" shaft hole. First sink the large-diameter hole to a depth of 1", then follow up with the 1"-diameter hole, and then finally tidy up with the large-sized bit (Fig 8-10).

11 Now have a trial fitting. The shaft needs to be a smooth-sliding fit through the chamber, the face of the spigot needs to be set back a little from the front rim of the chamber, and the whole works has to be a snug fit in the cradle (Fig 8-11).

12 Having marked on the front face of the spigot the size and position of the four gate slots, the tricky task of cutting them out comes. The best method is to first

FIGURE 8-9

When you have turned off the boss and the rings at the front of the spigot, spend time generally tidying up. Make a point of cleaning out the step so the back face of the spigot is at right angles to the shaft.

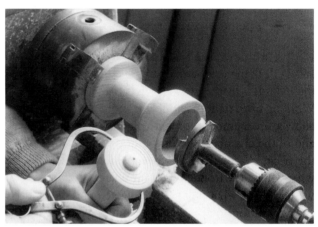

FIGURE 8-10

If you sink the hole in stages by repeatedly running the bit in and out, you will avoid burning the wood or the bit. Be careful when you exit that you don't throw the workpiece off-center.

FIGURE 8-11

Have a trial fitting. The chamber needs to be a tight-gripped fit in the cradle, while the shaft needs to be able to turn freely within the chamber.

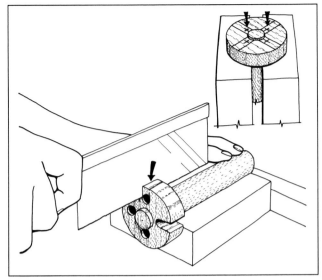

FIGURE 8-12

(top) With the spigot shaft well gripped and supported between a couple of wooden V-blocks, run the ⅜″-diameter drill holes all the way down through the thickness of the spigot end.

(bottom) Support the shaft in or on the V-block, and clear the waste with a small, fine-toothed gents or brass-backed handsaw.

clear the ends of the slots with the ⅜″-diameter drill—this establishes the width and depth of the slot—and then use the back saw to run parallel cuts from the rim of the spigot through to the drilled holes (Fig 8-12).

13 Finally, run two ½″-diameter holes through the rim of the chamber for the pipes, and cut a slice out of the handle end of the shank in readiness for fitting the crank with a tenon wedge.

TURNING THE PIPES AND BOSS RING

1 With the greater part of the project made, now is the time to look to the working drawing (Fig 8-1) and then perhaps to modify the unmade components. I say this because if your way of working is anything like mine, then chances are some part will need, in some way or other, to be reshaped or resized.

2 When you have a clear understanding of precisely how the remainder of the project needs to go, take the length of 1″ × 1″-square section wood, meaning the piece you have chosen for the pipes, and mount it in the lathe as already described.

3 Swiftly turn down the wood to a diameter of about ¾″, then take the ruler and dividers and mark all the step-offs that make up the design. It's beautifully easy; all you do is allow about ⅛″ for tailstock waste, and then mark eight ½″ step-offs.

4 With the step-off guidelines in place, take the skew chisel and round-nosed gouge and set to work systematically turning off all the little curves and grooves.

5 After turning the string of repeat cuts that make up the two little pipes, burn in the decorative V-cuts with the wire, and clean up with the skew chisel (Fig 8-13).

6 Finally, fit the ¼″ Forstner bit in the tailstock drill chuck, run a hole through the whole length of the turning and then part off.

7 With the two pipes made and off the lathe, use the scroll saw to swiftly cut a little disk blank of plum to size—it needs to be about ½″ thick and 1½″ in diameter—and mount it in the jaws of the chuck.

8 Now turn down one face of the blank to an accurate disk, reverse the disk in the chuck and turn the other face, round over the edge of the disk so you have a little domed shape. Drill the turning through with the ⅝″-diameter drill bit (Fig 8-14).

FIGURE 8-13

Use the toe of the skew chisel to set in the various steps and grooves.

FIGURE 8-14

Use the ⅝″ bit to run the hole all the way through the boss. If you are working in the way described, you should be able to run the bit through without touching the inside face of the chuck jaws.

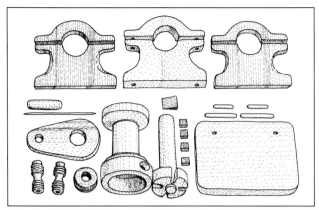

FIGURE 8-15
The component parts—all cut and ready for putting together.

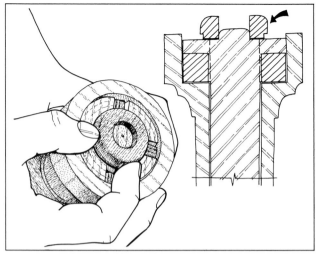

FIGURE 8-16
Set the ring on the boss so the gates are nicely contained; they need to be a loose, sliding fit.

9 Lastly, having first checked that the boss does in fact fit into the ring, rub it down with the graded sandpapers and take it off the lathe.

PUTTING TOGETHER AND FINISHING

1 Check the component parts for potential problems and make sure they fit together (Fig 8-15).

2 Cut the little sliding gate blocks to size, note how they fit in place, and generally rub down all the mating faces so the gates are a well-contained sliding fit.

3 Set the gates in the slots, and hold them in place with the boss ring (Fig 8-16); set the pipes in their holes; and set the crank handle on the end of the shaft (Fig 8-17).

4 Set the chamber in the cradle, and draw a couple of registration marks so you know what goes where and how (Fig 8-18). Generally pencil mark the position of the cradle on the base and the crank on the shaft so you will be able to complete the gluing stage without giving much thought to the positioning.

5 Finally, when you are pleased with the look and fit of the whole project, glue it together (Fig 8-19). Drill and fit the decorative dowel pegs (Fig 8-1), wipe the whole workpiece with the teak oil, and burnish it to a sheen finish.

PROBLEM SOLVING

■ If you are new to wood turning I strongly recommend you get a four-jaw chuck, a tailstock drill chuck, and a really good set of Forstner drill bits.

FIGURE 8-17
Set the pipes in the holes so they are aligned with the axis or center of the turning.

FIGURE 8-18
The chamber needs to be a tight-gripped fit between the cradle and the collar.

FIGURE 8-19
Glue fit the chamber in place in the cradle, and then glue mate surfaces and set the collar in position.

PROJECT NINE

Sector Wheel Bearing Machine

Color photo page 35

PROJECT BACKGROUND

Sector wheel bearings are, in many ways, at the very heart of engineering systems.

Sector wheels are the "wheels within wheels" that keep everything moving. Their primary function is to smooth out the operation by reducing friction, in much the same way as roller bearings and ball bearings. In fact, sector bearings were invented before all the rest; they were the prototype for bearings that were to follow.

The working movement of this machine is wonderfully simple and direct: As the crank handle is turned on the fixed pivot, the captured wheels within the sector frame will follow the fixed path defined by the edge of the pan (above).

PROJECT OVERVIEW

Have a good, long look at the working drawing (Fig 9-1) and the template design (Fig 9-2), and consider that, at a grid scale of two squares to 1″, the machine stands about 5″ in total height and 7″ across the diameter of the wheel pan.

The machine made up almost entirely of turned components—the pan, bearing wheels, handle and knobs.

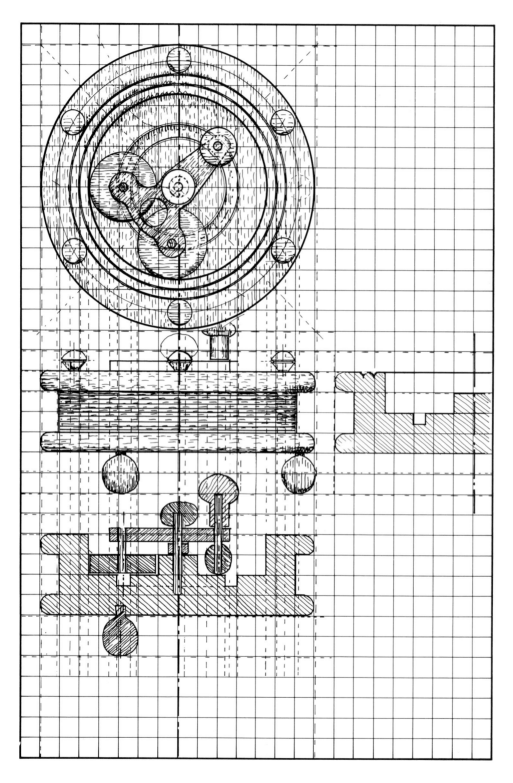

FIGURE 9-1
At a grid scale of two squares to 1″, the machine stands about 5″ high from the underside of the bun feet through to the top of the handle and about 7″ wide across the diameter of the pan.

PROJECT NINE: TEMPLATE DESIGN

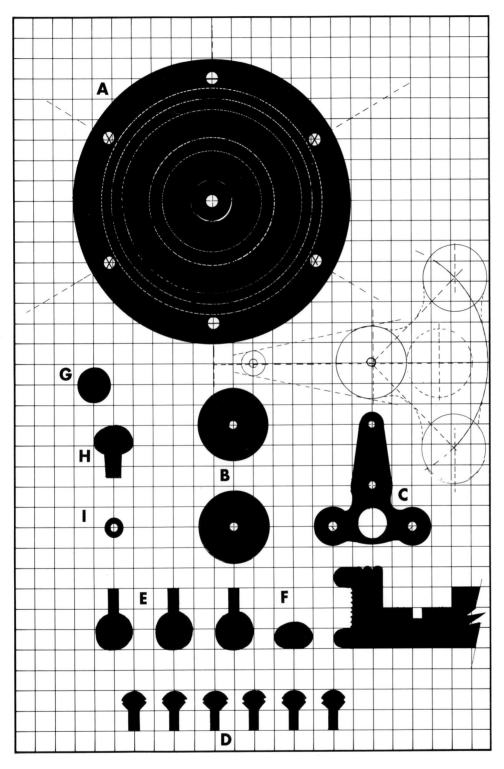

FIGURE 9-2
The scale is four grid squares to 1" for the black silhouettes and four squares to the inch for the line drawing.
A *Large pan.*
B *Bearing wheels.*
C *Sector frame.*
D *Decorative knobs (6).*
E *Buns (3).*
F *Bun knobs.*
G *Handle base.*
H *Handle.*
I *Washer.*

CUTTING LIST—PROJECT NINE

A	Large pan	2 × 8 × 8 maple or beech
B	Bearing wheels	2 × 2 cherry
C	Sector frame	3/8 × 4 × 4 cherry
D	Decorative knobs (6)	3/4 × 3/4 × 9 walnut
E	Buns (3)	1 1/4 × 1 1/4 × 10 beech
F	Bun knob	
G	Handle base	1 × 1 × 6 cherry
H	Handle	1 × 1 × 6 cherry
I	Washer	1 × 1 × 6 cherry
	Pivots and pegs	1/8" dowel (or round toothpicks)

CHOOSING YOUR WOOD

As with all the wood-turning projects, the wood must be easy to turn. The wood must be well seasoned, straight grained, and generally described as being easy to turn. We settled for maple for the large pan, North American cherry for the bearing wheels, American walnut for the decorative knobs, and beech for the feet.

MAKING THE PAN

1 Having studied the working drawing (Fig 9-1) and the template design (Fig 9-2), carefully selected your wood, and painstakingly planned the sequence of work so you know how to proceed, take the 2"-thick slab of maple—the piece for the base—and mark it with a 7"-diameter circle.

2 Cut out the blank on the band saw, and mount it on a 6"-diameter faceplate. Use short, fat screws at about 3/4" long for fixing, with about 3/8" of the screw going into the wood.

3 Mount the whole works on the lathe, set out all your tools so they are readily available, and check that you and the lathe are in good, reliable working order.

4 Position the tool rest over the bed of the lathe, and use a large gouge to swiftly turn down the blank to a smooth diameter of 7".

5 Mark the center point with the toe of the skew chisel, and then fix the dividers—first to a radius of 3/8" and then 1 3/4"—and mark the face of the wood with the various lines that make up the design (Fig 9-3). Move the tool rest out to the side of the lathe, and mark the band that runs around the edge of the wheel.

6 Use the parting tool and skew chisel to sink the 1 3/4"-wide wheel track to a depth of 1". Bring the whole area to a good, smooth, sharp-sided finish. The best working procedure is to first establish the depth at the sides and then to clean up the rest (Fig 9-4).

7 Continue turning the decorative beads that run around the rim, continue turning the edge and so on (Fig 9-5).

8 When you are happy with the profiles and finish, take a length of wire and friction burn the grooves that decorate the channel that runs around the edge of the pan (Fig 9-6). Warning: On no account should you wrap the wire around your fingers or have loop handles;

FIGURE 9-3
Use the ruler and dividers to mark the central pivot point, the width of the track, and the decorative band that runs around the turning.

FIGURE 9-4
Use the parting tool to lower the waste to the desired depth. Hold the tool so the inside face is at right angles to the bottom of the pan.

FIGURE 9-5
Use the tool of your choice to turn the decorative beads that run around the face of the pan. Note that I'm using an old file I've ground to a beaklike point.

use sticks so the wire can be swiftly released if there are snarls.

9 Finally, having first rubbed down all surfaces to a smooth finish, leave the turning on the faceplate, and take it off the lathe.

TURNING THE WHEELS

1 Take the length of 2"×2"-square wood you've selected for the wheels, establish the end center points by drawing crossed diagonals, and mount it securely on the lathe.

2 Having turned down the wood to the largest possible round section, use the dividers and parting tool to cut the two wheel thicknesses. Aim for two ½"-thick wheels at 1¾" diameter. The best approach is to clear the bulk of the rough with the gouge and then to use the skew chisel to shave the turning to a good fit and finish (Fig 9-7).

3 When you think the wheels are to size, carefully draw the tailstock out of the way, and have a trial fitting of the wheels in the pan (Fig 9-8). Be cautious that you don't knock the workpiece off-center.

4 With the wheel diameter ever-so-slightly smaller than the width of the pan track, rub down the wheels to a smooth finish, and part them off one piece at a time with the lathe (Fig 9-9). Note: If you have a tailstock drill chuck, you could bore out the pivot holes prior to parting off.

5 Lastly, having first run ⅛"-diameter holes through the wheel centers, mark the position of the wheel

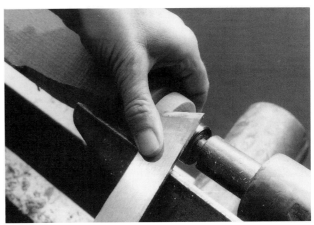
FIGURE 9-7
Use the left hand both to support the workpiece and to control the cutting pressure.

FIGURE 9-8
When you think the wheels are to size, stop the lathe, back the tailstock out of the way, and have a trial fitting. Aim to have a small space between the side of the heel and the center of the pan.

FIGURE 9-6
Firmly hold the copper wire on top of the spinning workpiece to friction burn a series of decorative rings. Warning: On no account should you wrap the wire around your fingers or have loop handles; you must be able to swiftly drop the wire if it starts to snarl.

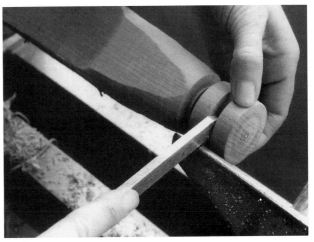
FIGURE 9-9
Having cleaned up the face of the first wheel, back the tailstock out of the way and carefully part off.

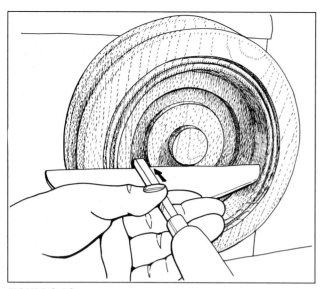

FIGURE 9-10
Use the parting tool to sink the channel at the bottom of the pan.

FIGURE 9-11
Turn down the cylinder so you have a beadlike string of little drum shapes. Note how the wood is securely held in the chuck and pivoted on a live tailstock center.

centers on the bed of the pan track. This done, remount the pan on the lathe, and mark the center-of-wheel line with a ½"-wide, ¼"-deep channel (Fig 9-10).

TURNING THE DECORATIVE KNOBS AND BUNS

1 First of all, have a look at the working drawing (Fig 9-1) and the project photographs, and see that there are six decorative knobs set at 60° intervals around the top rim of the pan and three knobs, or buns, set at 120° intervals around the underside of the base.

2 Feel free to change the shape and size of the turnings to suit your needs, select the length of wood for the decorative knobs, and mount it on the lathe.

3 With the wood securely mounted between the four-jaw chuck and the tailstock, turn it down to a diameter of about ½".

4 Use the dividers to mark the string of beadlike repeats that make up the six knobs. For ease of turning, I decided to stay with a ¼" module—¼" for the top of the knob, ¼" for the bottom, and ¼" for the stalk or spigot (Fig 9-11). Sink the waste, meaning the width of the spigot, to match one of your drill bit sizes. Aim for a diameter between ⅛" and ⅜".

5 With the little blanks all cut to size, take the skew chisel and set to work systematically turning them to the desired shape. Work along the turning in one direction and then rerun in the other direction. Turn off the bottom shoulder on all six forms, then cut in the decorative lines on all six forms (Fig 9-12).

FIGURE 9-12
Use the heel of the skew chisel to turn off the sharp shoulders. The best procedure is to work along the turning in one direction and then rerun in the other direction. If you have doubts about your turning skills, turn off more shapes than you need and select the choice set.

6 When you have achieved what you figure are six well-turned knobs, take the wire and mark each midline with a decorative, friction-scorched stripe.

7 Having first of all parted the knobs off the lathe with the toe of the skew chisel, set them one piece at a time in the jaws of the chuck, and sand the cutoff points to a smooth, rounded finish.

8 Have a look at the working drawing (Fig 9-1) and the various photographs, and see that we turned off four buns—three to be used as feet and one to be used as a support under the handle end of the little wheel frame.

9 Working in much the same way as already described, mount the wood on the lathe, turn it down to a cylinder, use the dividers to set out the step-offs that make up the design, reduce the waste at the spigot and so on until you have four identical little drum-shaped blanks (Fig 9-13).

10 To turn the buns to the roundish nutlike shape you should:
■ Set the skew chisel flat down on the workpiece so the heel is on the midline and looking in the direction of cut.
■ Gently rotate the tool until the blade begins to bite.
■ Lift and rotate so as to cut away the sharp shoulder. If you are doing it properly, the lifting-rolling action will cut off a ribbon of waste, while at the end of the pass, the tool should be in the valley with the toe uppermost.

11 Continue to repeatedly set the heel of the skew on the midline, lifting and rotating—first to the left to remove all the shoulders on one side and then to the right to remove the shoulders on the other side—until you finish up with four well-turned forms (Fig 9-14).

12 Sand each bun to a smooth finish, then part off the turnings from the lathe, remount them one at a time in the jaws of the chuck, and sand the part-off area to a smooth finish (Fig 9-15).

MAKING THE WHEEL SECTOR BEARING FRAME

1 First of all, have a good look at the working drawing (Fig 9-1) and the line drawing (Fig 9-2), and see how the form is drawn with a compass and ruler. Note how the main pivot point is set at the center of a large circle, while the bearing wheel centers are set on the circumference of the circle.

2 When you have a clear understanding of how to achieve the image, draw it on your chosen piece of ⅜"-thick wood so the center line runs in the direction of the grain.

3 Fix the position of the four holes, and run them through with the ⅛"-diameter drill bit. Then move to the scroll saw and fret out the profile. Being mindful that the speed of cut will change as you cut alternately with and across the grain, run the line of cut a little to the waste side of the drawn line.

4 Using a large-sized drill bit—or you could cut a hole on the scroll saw—reduce the weight and lighten up the appearance of the form by piercing the center area (Fig 9-16). Be careful not to weaken the structure by having the pierced window too near the edge of the profile.

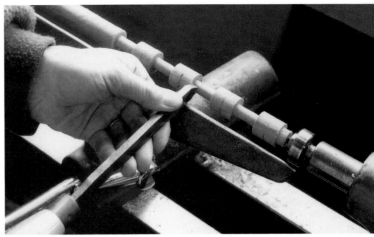

FIGURE 9-13
Use the parting tool to swiftly sink the areas of waste.

FIGURE 9-14
When you have achieved what you consider are a well-matched set of buns, tidy up the spigots with the parting tool, and use the toe of the skew chisel to very nearly part off the turnings one from another.

FIGURE 9-15
Hold the bun by its spigot, and use the sandpaper to rub down the part-off point to a smooth finish.

PUTTING TOGETHER AND FINISHING

1 When you have made all the component parts that make up the machine—the disk shape pan, two wheels, sector frame, and various decorative bits and knobs—check them over just to make sure they are free from damage, give them a light rubdown with the teak oil, and then clear the work surface to prepare for putting the pieces together (Fig 9-17).

2 Before you do anything else, especially if there is a likelihood that one of the component parts is made from suspect wood—it might be damp or have a knot or whatever—set the wheels in the frame and the frame on the main pivot, and try out the movement. If all is correct, the contact between the wheels and the inside face of the pan should be such that there is just enough friction to set the wheels in motion but not so much that they stick (Fig 9-18). If need be, take a fold of the finest-grade sandpaper and rub down the wheel rims to fit.

3 Glue the three bun feet and the six knobs in place, glue the main pivot in the center of the pan, glue the ends of the wheel pivots in the sector frame, fit and glue the handle in place, fit the wheels in the frame and the frame on the center pivot and so on until the task is done. And, of course, if and when you find that such and such a component part sticks or is deformed or whatever—which sooner or later you most certainly will—then be ready to ease and modify the offending part accordingly.

4 Finally, wipe away the dust, burnish the oiled surface to a sheen finish, and the machine is ready for action.

PROBLEM SOLVING

■ I think it fair to say that the innate character of this project is such that it needs to be made on the lathe. But what to do if you haven't a lathe? Well, if you are really keen, you could possibly seek out a lathe at the local school or join a group or build your own lathe.

■ Being mindful that as wood dries it shrinks across the width of the grain, this is all the more reason you must use well-seasoned wood for making disks and wheels. If you find that the wheels jam when you bring the machine into the house—even though they started out as a perfect fit—this is a good indication that the wood is still drying, shrinking and moving. Avoid using woods that are so inherently unstable that they never stop moving.

■ If at any point along the way you find that a component part splits or doesn't seem to want to come out right or looks wrong or whatever, always be ready to give it another try.

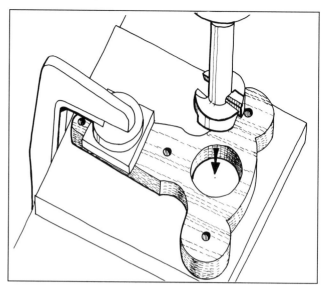

FIGURE 9-16
Being careful not to get too near the edge of the profile, use a large-sized drill bit to bore out the pierced window.

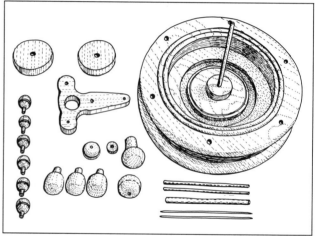

FIGURE 9-17
Set out all the component parts, and check them over for potential problems.

FIGURE 9-18
When you are ready for glue dip the points of round toothpicks, wedge the points in loose-fit holes, make adjustments for a good fit, and trim back when the glue is dry.

Flywheel Propeller Machine

Color photo page 36

PROJECT BACKGROUND

This machine is made up of two key engineering devices, namely, a flywheel and a propeller. Flywheels must surely be one of the most commonly used engineering mechanisms of all time; they are everywhere . . . in clocks, in automobiles, in motors, and in just about everything from toys and tools to tram cars and traction engines.

The dictionary says of a flywheel: "A flywheel is a heavy wheel that stores kinetic energy and smooths the operation of a reciprocating engine by maintaining a constant speed of rotation over the whole cycle" (above).

PROJECT OVERVIEW

Have a good long look at the working drawing (Fig 10-1a) and the template design (Fig 10-1b). Note that the propeller boss, flywheel, bell-shaped distance hubs at either side of the flywheel, pull cord ring, and ball stop at the end of the shaft are all turned.

If you don't have a lathe, you can modify the forms and make them from flatwood cutouts. The efficiency of the movement hinges primarily on the flywheel's precision and any nonturned modifications must be made with extra special care.

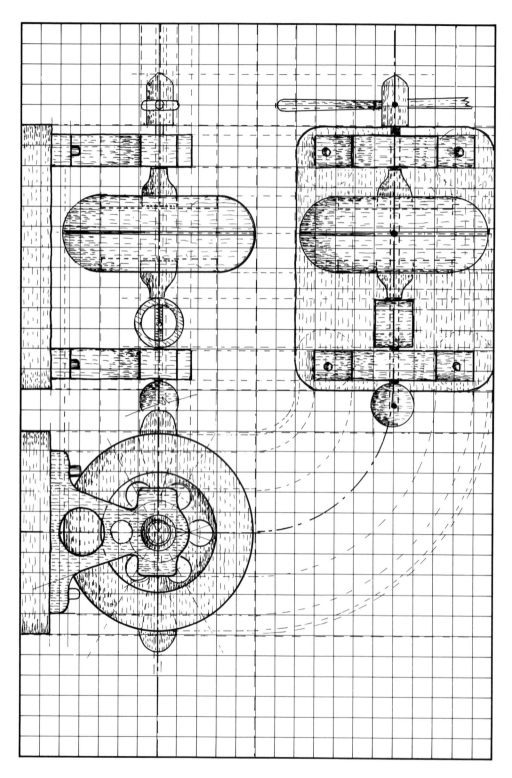

FIGURE 10-1A
At a grid scale of two squares to 1", the machine stands 6" high from the underside of the base through to the top of the flywheel, about 9" long, and about 6" wide across the span of the propeller.

PROJECT TEN: TEMPLATE DESIGN

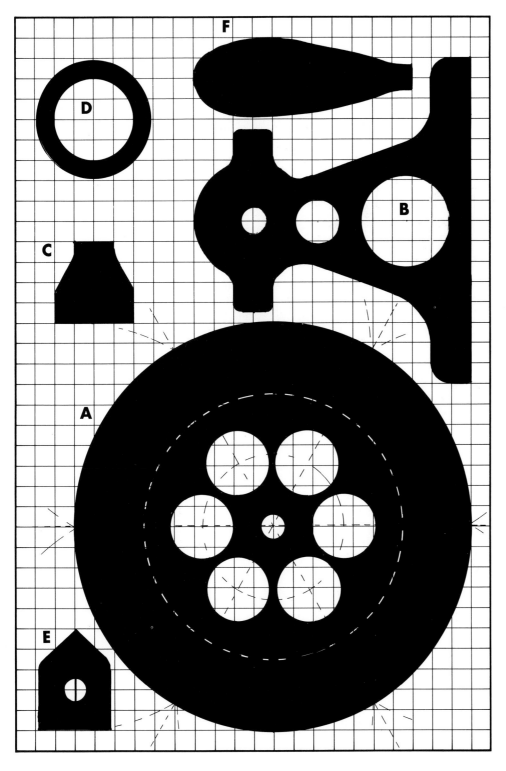

FIGURE 10-1B
The scale is four grid squares to 1". Note that the position of the six holes on the flywheel is fixed with a compass.
A *Flywheel.*
B *Stanchions (2).*
C *Spacers (2).*
D *Pull ring.*
E *Boss.*
F *Propellers.*

CUTTING LIST—PROJECT TEN	
A Flywheel	2 × 6 × 6 maple
B Stanchions (2)	¾ × 8 × 9 cherry
C Spacers (2)	1¼ × 1¼ cherry
D Pull ring	1¾ × 1¾ cherry
E Boss	1 × 1 beech
F Propellers	2—¼ × 1 × 3 beech
Base	¾ × 5 × 6½ beech
Ball stop	1 × 1
Main shaft	9"—⅜" dowel
Pegs	6"—¼" dowel
Fixing pins	round toothpicks

CHOOSING YOUR WOOD

Two considerations influenced our choice of wood: the need for the flywheel to be as heavy as possible and the fact that the wheel was going to be made on the lathe. We settled for European beech for the base slab, North American cherry for the stanchions and the small turnings, and North American maple for the flywheel.

MAKING THE BASE

1 Having studied the working drawing (Fig 10-1a) and template design (Fig 10-1b), take the ¾"-thick slab of beech—the piece for the base—and mark it with all the measurements that make up the design.

2 Cut the base to size with your chosen tools and sand it down to a smooth finish.

3 Have another look at the working drawing (Fig 10-1a) so you know what goes where and how, and then use a soft pencil, ruler and square to mark the base with all the guide- and placement lines. For example, label the propeller end, draw in an end-to-end center line, establish the position of the two stanchions and so on.

MAKING THE STANCHIONS

1 Take your chosen piece of wood and transfer the lines of the design from the working drawings through to the wood. Tip: I usually draw the design up to full size on the work-out paper, make a tracing, and then use the tracing to establish the primary reference points. Some woodworkers paste a paper pattern on the wood and then cut through the paper, wood and all.

2 Use the scroll saw to cut out the profiles.

3 Mark the position of the three holes: the ⅜"-diameter shaft hole and the other two holes at ½" and 1⅛" diameters.

4 When both cutouts have been identically marked, run the holes through on the drill press. It's important from workpiece to workpiece that the shaft holes are the same distance up from the baseline, so spend time getting it right.

5 Pencil label the stanchions for the propeller end and which direction the faces are looking.

TURNING THE FLYWHEEL

1 Take your 2"-thick slab of wood, fix the center point by drawing crossed diagonals, and then use the compasses/dividers to mark it with a circle at a little over 5" in diameter (Fig 10-2a).

2 Cut out the blank on the band saw, and mount it on a 3"-diameter screw chuck.

3 Mount the whole works on the lathe, and check that you and the lathe are in good, safe working order.

4 Position the tool rest over the side of the lathe, and use a large gouge to swiftly turn down the blank to a smooth diameter of a little over 5".

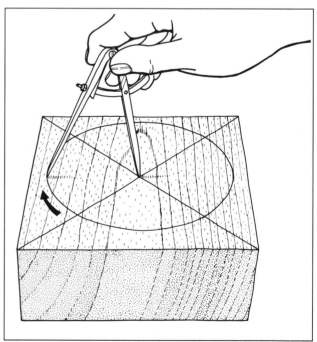

FIGURE 10-2A

Fix the center of the slab by drawing crossed diagonals, draw out the circle, and then clear the waste with the band saw.

5 Move the rest over the bed of the lathe so you can work the wood face on, and use your chosen tools to turn off the face of the disk.

6 Mark the center point with the toe of the skew chisel; then fix the dividers to a radius of about 1⅝″, and mark the face of the wood with a 3¼″-diameter circle. Note: The circle must be slightly bigger than the diameter of your screw chuck.

7 Use the parting tool and skew chisel to sink and waste the center of the disk to a depth of at least ¼″. Bring the whole central area to a good, smooth finish.

8 Use the gouge and skew chisel to round over the edge so you have a radius curve of about ⅞″ (Fig 10-2b).

9 Having turned down one radius curve, flip the tool over, and start the curve on the other side of the wheel (Fig 10-3).

10 Spend time cleaning up one side of the turning (Fig 10-4) so the profile is crisp and sharp, and then record the diameter of the sunken area with the dividers (Fig 10-5). Turn the wood over on the screw chuck, and rerun the whole procedure on the other side.

11 When you have what you consider is a nicely turned flywheel, rub it down to a smooth finish, and take it off the lathe.

12 Use the compasses to position the six holes, and drill them with a ¾″-diameter Forstner bit. Lastly, drill out the central ⅜″-diameter shaft hole (Fig 10-6).

FIGURE 10-2B
Use the skew chisel to cut the quarter-circle curve that runs from the center line and around to the rim of the sunken area. I use the side of the skew chisel like a scraper; it's not very good for the cutting edge, but it gets the job done without the need for changing tools.

FIGURE 10-4
Use the parting tool to clean up the edge of the sunken area.

FIGURE 10-3
When you have completed the curve at one side, turn the skew chisel so it's nose down, and tidy up the V-section midline.

FIGURE 10-5
Before you turn the workpiece over on the screw chuck and work the other side, use the dividers to take a radius reading.

TURNING THE BELL-SHAPED SPACERS

1 Have a look at the working drawing (Fig 10-1a) and template design (Fig 10-1b), and see that— apart from the flywheel—there are five secondary turnings: two bell-shaped distance spacers—one at either side of the flywheel—a ring that holds the pull string, a boss for the propeller blades, and a ball stop at the back end of the shaft.

2 Take your piece of wood for the two bell-shaped spacers and turn it down to a diameter of 1".

3 Use the dividers to mark the cylinder with all the step-offs. Allow a small amount at each end for chuck waste, 1" for each of the spacers, and about ¼" at center for part-off waste (Fig 10-7).

4 Study the shape of the bell (Fig 10-1b), then use the small, round-nosed gouge and the skew chisel to turn down the two little forms to shape (Fig 10-8).

5 Rub down the turnings to a smooth finish, part them off from the lathe, and run them through with a ⅜"-diameter hole—a hole to match the diameter of your shaft.

TURNING THE PULL STRING RING

1 Mount your chosen length of wood on the lathe— we use a four-jaw chuck—and swiftly turn it down to a diameter of about 1½" (Figs 10-1a and b).

2 Use the dividers to scribe the 1" length. Mark a center line with the toe of the skew chisel, and part off from the tailstock.

FIGURE 10-6

Having used a compass to fix the position of the six holes, set the flywheel on a disk of waste wood, and run the holes through with a ¼" bit. Note how everything needs to be well clamped and secure.

3 With the workpiece still secure in the jaws of the four-jaw chuck, mount a 1"-diameter Forstner bit in a drill chuck at the tailstock end of the lathe, and run a 1"-diameter hole through your turning (Fig 10-9).

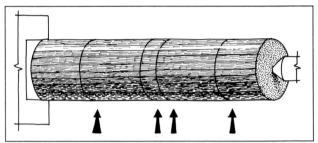

FIGURE 10-7

When you have achieved the 1"-diameter cylinder, use the dividers to mark the step-offs. Allow a small amount on each end for chuck waste, 1" for each of the turnings, and about ¼" at the center for part-off waste.

FIGURE 10-8

If your workpiece is supported in a chuck, you will be able to cut the turnings one piece at a time from the lathe. Note the way that we achieve symmetry by turning the two items as mirror-image profiles. The idea is that we move swiftly backward and forward from side to side, all the while making sure each stage is well matched.

FIGURE 10-9

Drilling out the ring using a tailstock chuck and Forstner bit, advance the tailstock at a steady rate, every now and again pulling back to clear away the waste shavings.

4 Now rub down the turning to a smooth finish, and part off from the lathe.

5 Lastly, using the center line as a guide, and being sure to drill across the grain, run a ⅜"-diameter hole through the ring—down through one side and on down through the other (Fig 10-10).

TURNING THE PROPELLER BOSS AND MAKING THE BLADES

1 Mount your carefully selected length of 1" × 1"-square wood, securely on the lathe.

2 Before you go any further, have a look at the various drawings and photographs, and see that the boss is only partially turned—at the nose and the corners—with the sides being left flat. The idea is that the propeller blades can be more easily fitted if they are located on flats.

3 When you have a clear understanding of just how the wood is to be worked, swiftly turn off the corners of the 1" × 1"-square section.

4 Having used the dividers to mark a single 1½"-long step-off, take the skew chisel and turn down one end of the workpiece to a smooth, round-nosed, or dome, finish. Make the nose about ½" long and the flats about 1" long (Fig 10-11).

5 Bring the turning to a good, smooth finish, and part off from the lathe. This done, sink a ⅜"-diameter hole into the flat end of the boss—to a depth of about ½"—and run a ¼"-diameter hole through one flat side and out of the other.

6 Finally, when you have considered the shape of the propeller blades (Fig 10-1b), take a knife and a couple of lengths of wood at about ¼" thick by 1" wide by 3" long and whittle the blades to shape and size. Aim for a couple of well-matched paddle-blade shapes (Fig 10-12).

PUTTING TOGETHER AND FINISHING

1 When you have made all the component parts that make up the machine—the base slab, two stanchions, flywheel, two spacers, pull cord ring, boss, propeller blades, and all the little dowel pegs and pins—then comes the fun task of putting everything together (Fig 10-13).

2 Start by dry fitting and pegging the two stanchions in place on the base. Set the propeller end stanchion in place, and then slide the shaft through the bearing, and make sure it runs free and easy.

FIGURE 10-10
Although, as the photograph shows, we ran the hole straight through the ring, it's really best to support the ring by sliding it on a length of waste dowel.

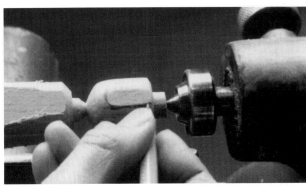

FIGURE 10-11
Turn down the square section so there are unturned ½"-wide flats on all four sides.

FIGURE 10-12
Use a sharp knife and a safe thumb-braced cutting action to whittle the blades to shape and size.

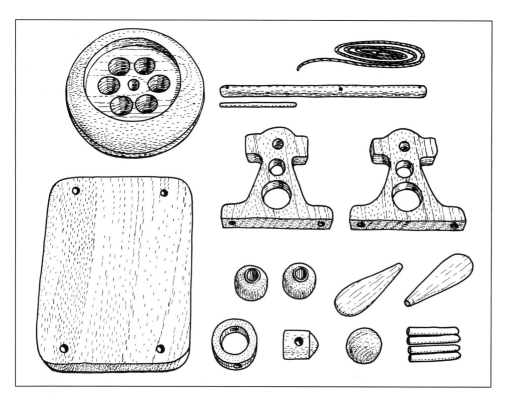

FIGURE 10-13
When you have completed all the component parts that make up the project, give them a good rubdown with the finest-grade sandpaper and a swift wipe with the teak oil. Be careful not to get the oil on surfaces that are to be glued.

FIGURE 10-14
Peg the first stanchion in place, and slide the shaft and the first spacer in position.

FIGURE 10-15
Do your best to see that the fixing pin runs between rather than across the holes.

3 Make sure the shaft is a smooth, accurate fit, then slide the other component parts on the shaft, drilling and pegging as you go. From the boss end, the order goes front stanchion, spacer, flywheel, spacer, pull string ring and back stanchion (Figs 10-14, 10-15, 10-16 and 10-17).

4 Check the spacing and the movement, and if need be, rub down the shaft or the holes until everything is a smooth fit. You might also have to reduce the length of one or both of the bell-shaped spacers.

5 With all the components in place on the shaft, spend time adjusting for best fit. Make sure the pin-fixing holes run through the center of both the component and the shaft.

6 Fit the boss and angle the propeller blades in the boss so they look like fan blades (Figs 10-18 and 10-19).

7 When everything is a good fit, pass the end of the cord through the pull hole and have a tryout. All

FIGURE 10-16
Cut off the flywheel pin so the wheel is able to turn, and slide the other spacer in position.

FIGURE 10-17
Slide the pull ring in place, and then follow up with the second stanchion.

you do is wind the string good and tight around the shaft, firmly hold the base on the work surface—with your knuckles well clear of the flywheel—and then give a good, smooth pull on the cord. If all is well, the flywheel will spin into action and then carry on spinning.

8 Lastly, when you are pleased with the running action, glue and peg everything into place, and give the whole works a swift wipe with the teak oil. Now the machine is finished and ready for action.

PROBLEM SOLVING

■ If you like the idea of this project but can't get use of a lathe, you could use shop-bought items for the turned parts: a large, wooden wheel for the flywheel; a length from the end of a broomstick for the boss; large, wooden beads for the spacers and end stop and so on.

■ If you decide to use a different wood for the flywheels, make sure it is a good weight and strong across the grain. In the context of this project, avoid loose, lightweight wood like jelutong and ragged, knotty wood like pine.

■ Be careful not to get the glue on areas that are to be oiled or oil on areas that are to be glued.

■ If by chance your flywheel fixing hole runs across one of the six large holes, making the round toothpick visible, then glue the round toothpick in place, and cut away the bit when the glue is set.

■ If you have a tailstock drill chuck, you could maybe modify the order of work and drill out the bell-shaped spacers while they are still on the lathe.

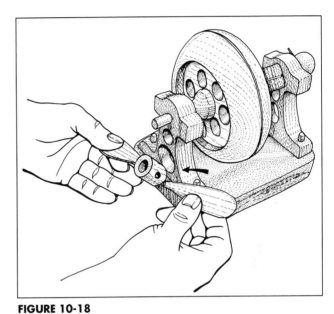

FIGURE 10-18
Trim the propeller blade ends to a tight push fit, and glue them in place in the boss holes.

FIGURE 10-19
Finally, glue fix the boss and the tail ball with round toothpicks, and trim back when the glue is dry.

Pyramid Roller-Ball Machine

Color photo page 37

PROJECT BACKGROUND

The sphere, or ball, is perhaps one of the most perfect and dynamic of all forms. Wheels, disks, spheres, balls and all circle-related forms are complete, self-contained and full of energy.

This machine is made up of thirteen balls: three groups of three small balls, pivoted and captured in the base frame, all topped off by four loose, larger balls. In use, the handle is turned, with the overall effect that the three balls on the drive shaft revolve and in so doing set all the other balls in motion (above).

PROJECT OVERVIEW

Have a good, long look at the working drawing (Fig 11-1) and the template design (Fig 11-2), and consider how this machine beautifully illustrates a number of key engineering principles that have to do with bearings, friction drive and movement. And, of course, it is also a machine that poses a number of pretty gritty engineering questions. For example, can you guess what direction the top balls will roll if you turn the handle counter-clockwise? Or what will happen if you top off the whole stack of balls with yet another ball?

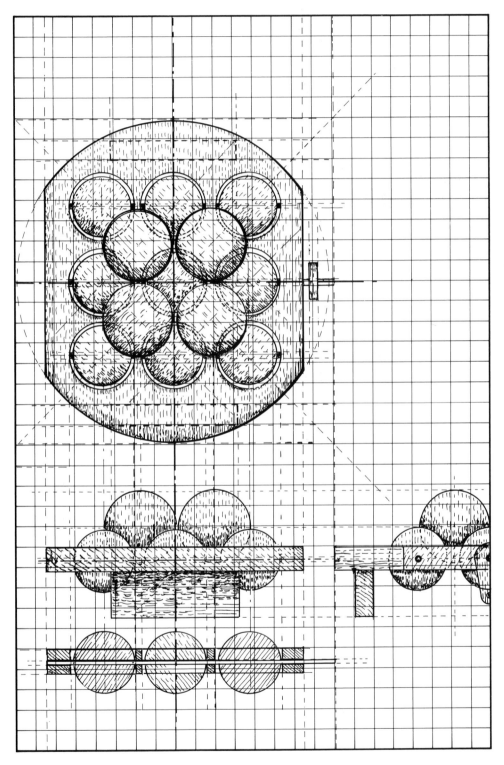

FIGURE 11-1
At a grid scale of two squares to 1", the machine stands about 4" high and 6⅜" across the flats of the frame.

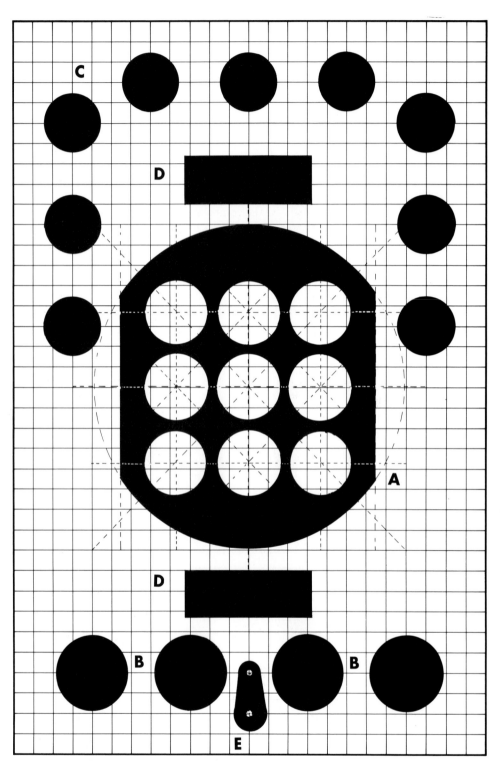

FIGURE 11-2
The scale is two grid squares to 1".
A *Base frame.*
B *Large balls (4).*
C *Small balls (9).*
D *Foot bars (2).*
E *Handle crank.*

CHOOSING YOUR WOOD

This project calls primarily for three wood types: a strong, heavy, tight-grained wood for the base frame; a lightweight, easy-to-turn wood for the nine small balls; and a heavy, easy-to-turn wood for the four large balls. We settled for using European beech for the frame and the four large balls—beech is both heavy and easy to turn—and jelutong for the nine small balls.

MAKING THE BASE FRAME

1 After looking at the working drawing (Fig 11-1) and template design (Fig 11-2), selecting your wood, and just as carefully planning out the order of work, take the $5/8''$-thick slab of beech—the piece for the base—and fix the center by drawing crossed diagonals. This done, use the compass to mark the slab with an $8''$-diameter circle.

2 Cut out the circle with your chosen tool. Now mount it securely on the faceplate. Use short, fat screws to minimize damage (Fig 11-3).

3 Mount the whole works on the lathe, set out all your tools so they are readily available, and check that you and the lathe are in good, safe working order.

4 Position the tool rest at an angle to the bed of the lathe, and use a large gouge to swiftly turn down the blank to a smooth diameter of $8''$.

5 Move the rest over the bed of the lathe so you can work the wood face on, and use your chosen tools to turn off the face and edge of the disk. Aim for an edge that is nicely rounded over at the working face (Fig 11-4).

6 When you are happy with the disk, rub it down to a smooth finish, mark the center point with the toe of the skew chisel, and take the disk off the lathe.

7 Use the compasses, square and ruler to draw all the lines that make up the design (Fig 11-2) and to fix the precise position of the nine holes. Be sure to have the straight sides aligned with the run of the grain.

8 Having made sure that all is correct, run the holes through with a $1\frac{3}{4}''$-diameter Forstner bit (Fig 11-5). It's important the holes are well placed and cleanly cut.

9 With all nine holes well placed and cleanly cut, run the disk through the band saw, and slice away the two areas of part-circle waste.

10 And now for the most difficult part of the project! If you look at the working drawing (Fig 11-1) and template design (Fig 11-2), you will see that the whole notion of giving the base frame two flat edges—edges that are perfectly square and parallel to each other—has to do with the actual procedure of drilling the pivot holes through the thickness of the wood. Without the edges,

FIGURE 11-3
Align the faceplate with the center point, and screw it securely in place. Try to place the screws so they occur in areas of waste, which are to be cut away.

FIGURE 11-4
Turn down the disk to a smooth, round-edged finish.

FIGURE 11-5
Run the holes through with the $1\frac{3}{4}''$ Forstner bit.

FIGURE 11-6

Having first made sure the workpiece is standing square and true—so the drill bit is perfectly aligned with the face of the wood—carefully run the pivot rod holes down through the thickness.

how else could you make sure the holes are aligned?

11 When you have made sure the edges are parallel and marked as many guidelines as you think necessary, fit the ¼″ bit in the drill, set the workpiece on edge—with blocks and clamps—and run the pivot holes down through the wood so they are well placed in the thickness of the wood and they run across the centers of the holes (Fig 11-6).

12 Still working on the drill press, sink a ¾″-wide, ¼″-deep stopped hole at the intersections between the holes.

13 Take the hooked knife—or you might use a scoop or spoon gouge—and carve away the edges of the ¾″-diameter hole. Aim for a sculptured surface that runs in a smooth sweep from the top face of the frame down into the dip and up again (Figs 11-7 and 11-8).

14 Finally, when have you achieved a good-to-look-at frame, rub it down to a supersmooth finish, and cut the two little foot bars to fit.

TURNING THE NINE SMALL BALLS

1 Taking your length of 2″×2″-square section jelutong—the length for the small balls—establish the end centers by drawing crossed diagonals, and mount it securely on the lathe.

2 With the wood at a smooth 1½″-diameter cylinder, set the dividers to 1½″ and step off all the guidelines that make up the design. Starting at the chuck, allow ¼″

FIGURE 11-7

Use a hooked knife to carve the smooth-curved dips at the intersections. Be careful not to cut through into the pivot rod holes.

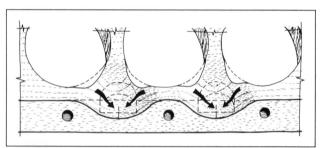

FIGURE 11-8

Cross section showing the depth of the carved dips.

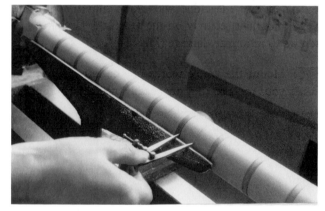

FIGURE 11-9

Mark the cylinder with all the divider step-offs that make up the design. Note how you can just about see in the photograph at top right, on the drawing, that we considered giving the frame extra legs and topping the four balls with another ball.

for chuck waste, 1½″ for the first ball, ¼″ for waste, 1½″ for the second ball, ¼″ for waste and so on along the length of the wood. Now reset the dividers to ¾″ and mark each step-off with a midline (Fig 11-9).

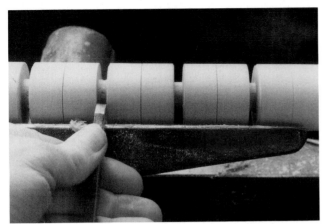

FIGURE 11-10
Use the parting tool to sink the waste to a depth of about ½".

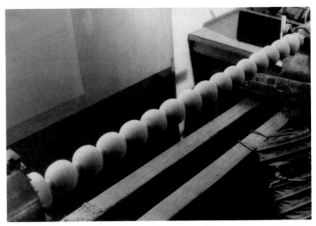

FIGURE 11-11
Do your best to make sure the string of balls are well matched.

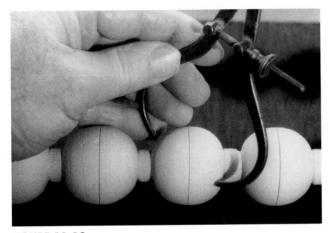

FIGURE 11-12
Use the calipers to check the turnings. Note that at this stage, the balls look to be slightly egg shaped.

3 Take the parting tool and sink the bands of between-ball waste to a depth of ½" so you are left with a central core at about ½" (Fig 11-10).

4 When you are happy with the markings, take the skew chisel and turn down the ball shapes. The sequence of work along the length of the wood is:
- Hold the skew chisel flat on the workpiece—on the midline—on the first ball nearest the headstock such that the heel is looking toward the headstock.
- Lift the handle until the blade begins to bite, and then advance in a smooth rolling action.
- Repeat the cut—from midline and down into the valley—until the ball begins to take shape.
- Having turned down one half of the ball, move on to the next ball in line, and rerun the action.
- When you have turned down the left-hand side of every ball, go back to the first ball in line, flip the chisel over so the heel is looking toward the tailstock, and then rerun the sequence of cuts for the other side of the balls.

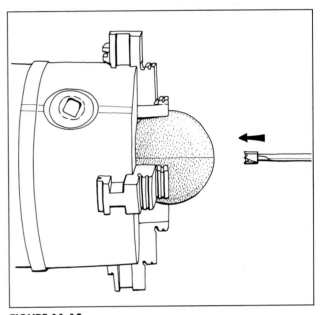

FIGURE 11-13
Drill out the ¼"-diameter pivot hole; use the turned midline as an alignment guide.

5 When you have turned the whole string of balls more or less to shape (Fig 11-11), go back to the first ball in line, and use the calipers (Fig 11-12) and skew chisel—and maybe also a cardboard template—and fine-turn each ball to the best possible shape and finish.

6 Take the whole string off the lathe and use a fine-bladed saw to cut the balls apart.

7 Take the balls one at a time, set them in the jaws of the chuck, and rub down the part-off points.

8 Finally, one piece at a time, hold the balls in the chuck—this time with the midline in the horizontal plane—and use the tailstock drill chuck and the ¼"-diameter bit to sink the pivot holes (Fig 11-13).

TURNING THE LARGE BALLS

1 The main difference between the small and large balls is not so much in the shape—although the small balls can be slightly flat faced at the holes—but more in the turning technique. For example, the small balls are turned off as a string, while the large balls are turned off one at a time.

2 Having mounted the wood on the lathe, cut a cardboard template, and marked off the sequence of step-offs (Fig 11-14)—all as already described in the previous section—lower the waste at either side of the ball at the tailstock end.

3 With the diameter of the midline defined by the width of the cylinder and the diameter across the poles defined by the bands of waste, all you have to do now is turn off the shoulders with the skew chisel, as already described.

4 Having more or less turned off the ball nearest the tailstock—first one half and then the other—and checked it with the cardboard template (Fig 11-15), wind back the tailstock so you can approach the ball end on, and carefully bring the ball to the best possible finish (Fig 11-16).

5 Finally, part off the ball with the toe of the skew chisel, wind back the tailstock so the workpiece is once again supported at both ends, and rerun the sequence for the other three balls.

PUTTING TOGETHER AND FINISHING

1 When you've completed all the component parts that make up the project—the base frame, two foot bars, nine small balls, four large balls, little crank bar and pivot rods—spread them out on the surface, and check them over for potential problems (Fig 11-17). Pay particular attention to the movement of the small balls on the pivot rods. The three central balls need to be a tight fit on the drive rod with the rod being a loose fit through the frame holes, while the outside balls need to be an easy-to-turn, loose fit on the rods with the rods being a tight fit in the frame holes.

2 Start by gluing and pegging the foot bars in place on the underside of the frame.

3 When the glue is dry, take the finest-grade sandpaper and spend time rubbing down the whole frame to a smooth finish (Fig 11-18). Pay particular attention to the carved dips on the top and the inside edges of the nine holes. Make sure the pivot holes are clean and free from jags.

FIGURE 11-14
Use the skew chisel to shave the wood to a good, smooth finish.

FIGURE 11-15
Use a cardboard template to check the profile.

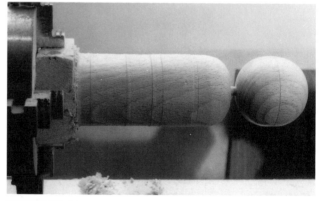

FIGURE 11-16
With the workpiece still held firmly and securely in the jaws of the chuck, back the tailstock out of the way and turn down the end face of the ball to a good profile and finish.

4 Having sanded the pivot rods so the balls are an easy-to-turn fit, fit the nine balls in place. The best procedure is to slide the rods through both the frame and the balls, fitting and easing as you go. Continue fitting

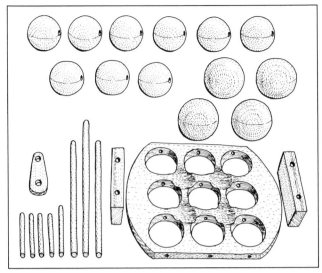

FIGURE 11-17
Set out all the component parts, and check them over for shape and size and possible faults.

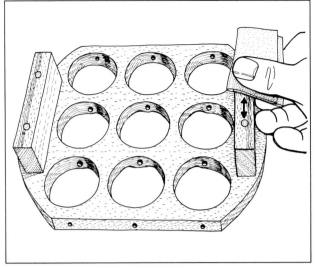

FIGURE 11-18
Having pegged and glued the foot bars in position and waited for the glue to dry, clean up the surface with a fold of sandpaper.

and modifying until everything comes together. For example, you might fit one ball, then decide that another is a better fit, then spend time sanding a ball so it turns freely (Fig 11-19) and so on.

5 When you have fitted all nine balls and their pivot rods in place and glued the little crank handle on the central rod, give the whole works a rubdown with teak oil, and burnish to a dull, sheen finish.

6 Finally, set the four large balls in place, turn the handle, and watch the movement of the balls as they revolve.

PROBLEM SOLVING

■ If you like the idea of this project but can't get use of a lathe, you could use shop-bought balls and settle for making only the frame.

■ If you decide to use a different wood for the balls, make sure it is a good weight, strong across the grain and suitable for turning.

■ Be careful not to get the glue on areas that need to revolve freely. A good tip is to generously oil everything except the faces that are to be glued before you start putting the parts together.

■ If you can't use a crooked knife, you could use a scoop gouge.

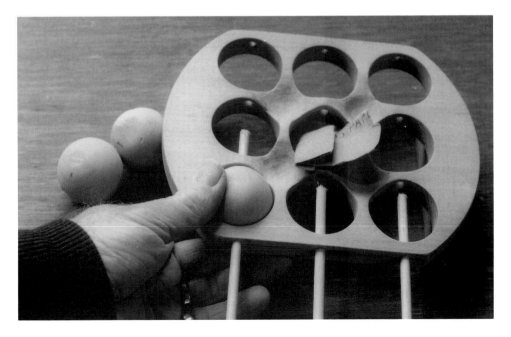

FIGURE 11-19
Experiment with the placement of the balls on the pivot rods until you achieve the best fit. If need be, use a fold of sandpaper to ease the fit.

Rack and Pinion Machine

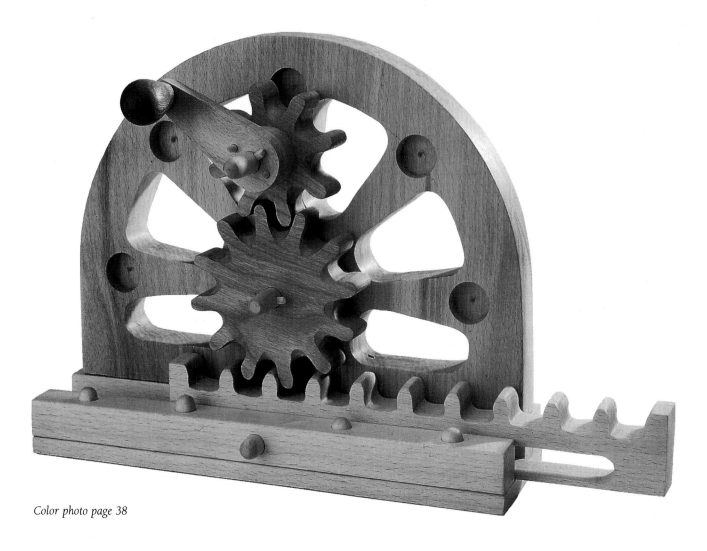

Color photo page 38

PROJECT BACKGROUND

This is one of our favorite projects. Rack and pinion is a device for converting rotary movement into linear motion and vice versa in which a gear wheel—the pinion—engages with a flat-toothed bar—the rack. When the crank handle is slowly turned—clockwise or counterclockwise—the cog wheel teeth engage, with the effect that the rack slides along its frame.

PROJECT OVERVIEW

Before you put tool to wood, have a good long look at the project picture (above), photographs, working draw-ing (Fig 12-1a) and template design (Fig 12-1b), and note that the machine is made up of three primary parts: a small gear wheel, large gear wheel, and long, toothed bar. Consider how the two wheels are pivoted on dowel shafts, with the smaller wheel being operated by a crank and handle. See that while the rack needs to be a nice, smooth-sliding fit between the bed rails, it also has to be held captive by means of a dowel rod that runs through the front rail, through a slot in the rack, and on through into the back rail.

PROJECT TWELVE: WORKING DRAWING

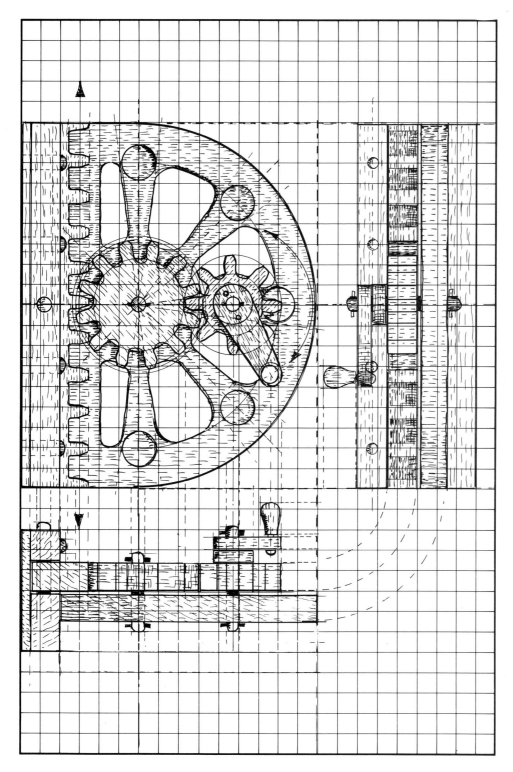

FIGURE 12-1A
At a grid scale of two squares to 1″, the machine stands 7¾″ high and 9″ wide. Note that in side view, the design primarily uses ¾″-wide stock.

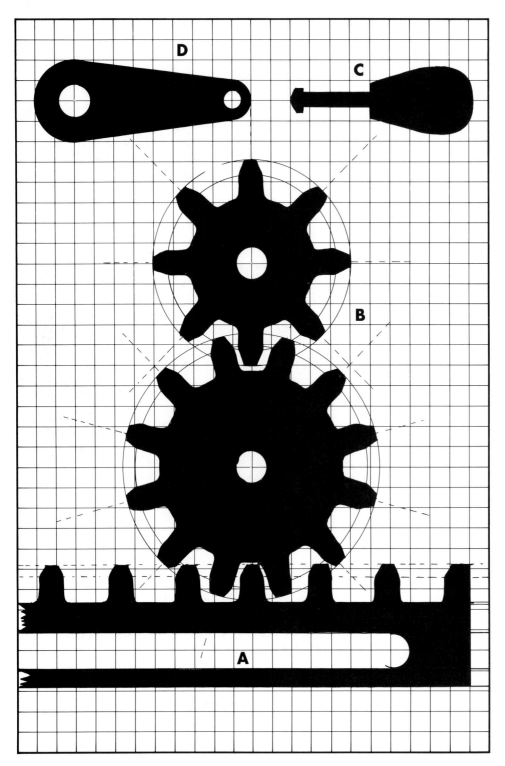

FIGURE 12-1B

The scale is four grid squares to 1". Although it is important you do your best to copy the profile and spacing of the teeth, we have shaped the design so there is plenty of leeway.

A *Rack.*
B *Wheels (2).*
C *Crank handle.*
D *Crank.*

CUTTING LIST—PROJECT TWELVE

A	Rack	¾ × 1½ × 9 beech
B	Wheels (2)	¾ × 4 × 6 cherry
C	Crank handle	1 × 1 × 6 walnut
D	Crank	¾ × 1 × 2¾
	Back plate	¾ × 9 × 7 beech
	Base	¼ × 3 × 9 beech
	Rails	¾ × 2 × 9 beech
	Washer	¾ × 1¼ × 1¼
	Rods	24"—⅜" dowel

CHOOSING YOUR WOOD

In this project the character of the wood is important. The wood for the gear wheels needs to be strong across the short grain, and must be smooth grained, free from knots, attractive in color, and easy to work.

We chose to use North American cherry for the wheels; European beech for the base, rails and back plate; North American walnut for the crank handle; and various offcuts for all the little bits and pieces.

MAKING THE BACK PLATE

1 Take the 7" length of ¾" beech at 9" wide. With the grain running from top to bottom, use the pencil, ruler, square and compasses to mark the lines that make up the design. We use an adjustable square and a washer for the radius curves. It's important the baseline is square and pivot points are correctly placed, so double-check everything (Figs 12-1a and b and 12-2).

2 Having shaded in all the areas that need to be cut away and pierced, use the drill and a suitably sized drill bit to drill pilot holes through all the enclosed "windows" of the design.

3 Now cut out the profile, making sure the blade is running slightly to the waste side of the drawn line.

4 When you cut out the enclosed "windows," the order of work is:
- Unhitch the scroll saw blade.
- Pass the blade through the pilot hole.
- Refit and retension the blade.

5 Now sand all inside radius curves to a good, smooth finish (Fig 12-3).

6 Use the ¾"-diameter Forstner bit to drill the five decorative blind holes that make up the design.

FIGURE 12-2

When you prepare to use the adjustable square to mark the design on the wood, make sure you start off with a square baseline and a reasonably smooth surface.

FIGURE 12-3

We use a small rotary carver—a small drum sander—to finish the difficult-to-reach, inside-radius curves.

Drill holes that are about ¼" deep (Fig 12-4).

7 Now smooth the back plate with sandpaper.

MAKING THE PINION GEAR WHEELS AND RACK

1 Trace the gear wheel and rack patterns on to your wood. It's important the teeth are accurately placed, so spend time getting it right.

2 Cut out the profiles on the scroll saw.

3 Check fit the wheels and movement (Fig 12-5). We used a couple of pencil stubs—and check out the movement by turning the wheels by hand. Make sure the three primary components, the two wheels and the rack, are a good, smooth-moving fit.

FIGURE 12-4
Forstner drill bits are perfect for sinking smooth-sided, flat-bottomed blind holes.

MAKING THE CRANK

1 Now draw out the washer spacer and crank. The washer needs to be 1″ in diameter. The crank is 2″ long from center to center, 1″ in diameter at the big end, and ½″ in diameter at the small end (Figs 12-1a and b).

2 With all the lines of the design clearly established, run ⅜″-diameter holes through the spacer washer and through the big end of the crank and a ¼″-diameter hole through the small end of the crank.

3 Use the scroll saw to cut out the two components.

4 When you have completed the two cutouts, both at ¾″ thick, run them through the band saw—or you might use the scroll saw—so you have two spacers and two cranks, all at about ⅜″ thick (Fig 12-6).

TURNING THE CRANK HANDLE AND MUSHROOM PIVOT

1 Take the 6″ length of 1″ × 1″-square section walnut, establish the end center points by drawing crossed diagonals, and mount it securely on the lathe.

2 Having checked through your safety checklist, turn down the wood to the largest possible diameter.

3 When you have completed a cylinder at about ⅞″ diameter, take the dividers and mark the cylinder with all the step-offs that make up the design. Working from the tailstock end, allow about ½″ for tailstock waste, 1¼″ for the handle, 1¼″ for the pivot stalk, ¼″ for the little mushroom head, and ¼″ for part-off waste (Fig 12-7).

4 Sink the step-offs to the required depth, and then turn the rounded shape of the handle, the ¼″-diameter stalk and the mushroom head.

FIGURE 12-5
Spend time making sure the three primary components, the two wheels and the rack, are a good, smooth-moving fit.

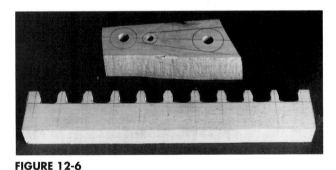

FIGURE 12-6
The use of ¾″-thick wood allows for two ⅜″ spacers and two ⅜″ cranks—one pair for this machine and one pair for another project.

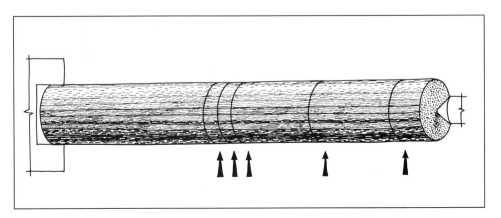

FIGURE 12-7
Working from the tailstock end, use the dividers to carefully mark the cylinder with all the step-offs that make up the design. Allow ½″ for tailstock waste, 1¼″ for the handle, 1¼″ for the pivot stalk, ¼″ for the mushroom-shaped head, and ¼″ for part-off waste.

FIGURE 12-8

When you have sanded to a good finish, use the toe of the skew chisel to part off the workpiece from the lathe.

5 Sand the turning and then part off so you have two components: the handle and pivot (Fig 12-8).

PUTTING TOGETHER AND FINISHING

1 Mount the backing plate on the base, position the two slide rails, and set the rack in place. When you are sure all is correct, drill and dowel (Fig 12-9).

2 With the rack a nice, smooth-running fit, set the two pinion wheels in place with a couple of temporary dowels, and test out the movement. Turn the small wheel, and mark any teeth that look to be a problem.

3 When you are happy with the movement, cut the dowel rods to size, drill peg holes, drill out the handle for the mushroom pivot, and sand over all the parts (Fig 12-10). Use round toothpicks for fixing everything in place.

4 With the back plate square to the base (Fig 12-11) and the rack free to move in its track, glue, fit, peg and clamp the project together and let it dry.

5 Finally, give the whole works a swift wipe with the teak oil; fit and peg the wheels, dowels and handle; and the machine is finished.

PROBLEM SOLVING

■ If you want to make the project but can't get use of a lathe, settle for making the crank handle from a shop-bought dowel.

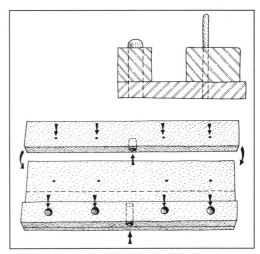

FIGURE 12-9

Place and align the base components so they are true to each other, and drill out the various fixing holes.
(top) Cross section.
(bottom) Plan view showing position of holes.

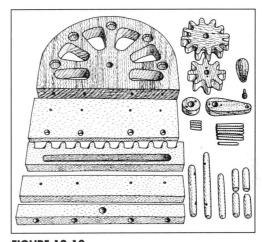

FIGURE 12-10

Check the component parts for potential problems.

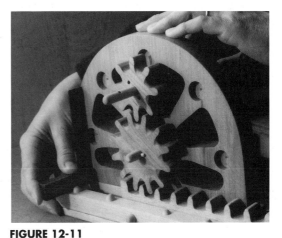

FIGURE 12-11

Be sure to check that the back plate is square to the base.

Pendulum Recoil Escapement Machine

PROJECT BACKGROUND

The tick, tick, ticking that measures time passing—is controlled in the traditional clock by a mechanism known as the pendulum recoil escapement. This wonderfully simple device is made up of a toothed wheel on a pivot, a pivoted anchorlike form we term an anchor escapement, a swinging weight on an arm we call a pendulum, and a falling weight that acts in much the same way as a spring.

The working movement is beautifully simple: As the toothed wheel is set into motion by the falling weight, or "spring," and the pendulum is set swinging, the clawlike pallet fingers at the end of the anchor and the teeth of the wheel all complement each other in keeping the machine in motion. One side of the swinging anchor gives a little push or recoil on the wheel teeth that in turn gives a little push on the other side of the anchor that in turn gives another push on the next wheel tooth and so on. In this manner, the movement is paced by the recoil energy as it bounces backward and forward between the two components. Of course, there is a great deal more to it than that, and if you are interested, go to a book on horology and refer to "pendulum recoil escapement."

PROJECT OVERVIEW

The size of the pendulum, the length of the pendulum arm, and the size of the "spring" weight in relation to the swing of the pendulum are all critical factors that relate to the success of the movement. Get one or other of the factors wrong—too much or too little weight, not enough swing or whatever—and everything grinds to a halt. That said, if you have doubts about your skills, proceed anyway and view this whole project as a prototype—an adventure that will lead on to other things.

Color photo page 39

PROJECT THIRTEEN: WORKING DRAWING

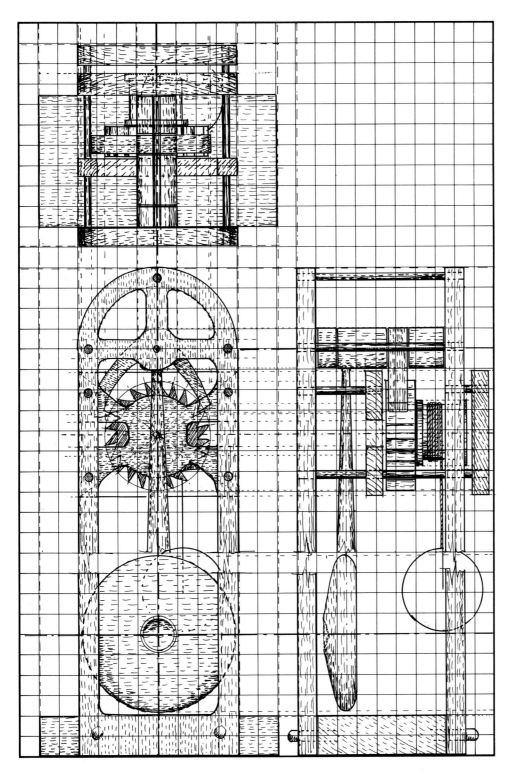

FIGURE 13-1
At a grid scale of two squares to 1", the machine stands about 15" high and 6" wide across the span of the base slab.

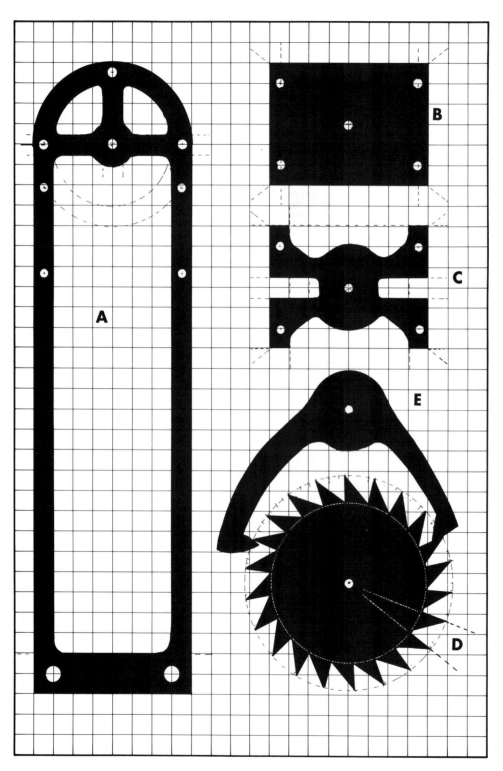

FIGURE 13-2
*The scale is two grid squres to
1" (A,B,C).*
*The scale is four grid squares to
1" (D,E).*
A *Tall, fretted frames (2).
Frames in between fretted
frames (2).*
B *Blank plate.*
C *Fancy plate.*
D *Toothed wheel.*
E *Anchor.*

CUTTING LIST—PROJECT THIRTEEN

A	Tall, fretted frames (2)	⅜ × 4 × 40 plum
	Frames in between fretted frames (2)	
B	Blank plate	⅜ × 4 × 3 plum
C	Fancy plate	⅜ × 4 × 3 plum
D	Toothed wheel	¾ × 2¾ × 2¾ beech
E	Anchor	½ × 2¼ × 3¼ beech
	Spacer drum (3)	1 × 1
	Base	¾ × 3¼ × 6 beech
	Pendulum arm	1 × 1 × 12 beech
	Pendulum weight	1 × 4 × 4 beech

CHOOSING YOUR WOOD

Being mindful that the woods variously need to be strong across the grain, close grained, free from knots, attractively colored, and relatively easy to work, we decided to go for European beech for the base and the pendulum; English plum for the frame; English beech for the toothed wheel, drum and anchor; and pine for the dowels. That said, you could use just about any wood type that takes your fancy, as long as you consider it structurally and technically fitting. For example, if you are trying to cut costs, you could use soft pine for the pendulum weight, arm, frame, and just about everything except the toothed wheel and anchor that need to be made from a close-grained, dense wood.

Note that we used a metal weight (a brass plum bob from an old level) for the "spring" for the simple reason that we couldn't find a lump of wood that was heavy enough.

MAKING THE FRETTED PLATES AND BASE

1 Have a good, long look at the working drawing (Fig 13-1) and the template design (Fig 13-2), and study the two views. Note that we have cut through the views—through the height—so they fit on the page. Study all the illustrations—the photographs and pen drawings—until you are completely clear in your own mind as to how the various parts of the project come together.

2 When you have an understanding of what goes where and how, draw the design imagery to size, make tracings, and transfer the traced lines through to your chosen wood. Note that in the context of the two identical frames—the two tall support frames—you need only draw the frame on one piece of wood.

3 Take the two lengths of wood that make up the two primary frames and pin them together so the drawn imagery is on the top layer.

4 On the drill press, use the ¼" bit to bore out the eight fixing-rod holes that occur at the top of the frame. Run the holes through both layers of wood. While the drill is in use, run ¼"-diameter pilot holes through all windows of waste and ⅜"-diameter holes through the bottom of the frame—for fixing the base.

5 Push dowels through at least two of the holes to ensure the holes and the cutouts are identically placed, and use the scroll saw to cut out the profiles.

6 To cut out the enclosed windows, the order of work is (Fig 13-3):
- Unhitch the scroll saw blade.
- Pass the blade through the pilot hole.
- Refit and retension the blade.
- Cut out the window.
- Reverse the procedure and remove the wood.

7 Having fretted through both layers of wood and removed the holding dowels, sand all the sawn edges—all the inside and outside radius curves and straight sides—to a smooth finish.

8 To cut the cradle plates that support the escapement, rerun the same procedures.

9 Cut the base slab to size, and have a trial fitting of the two main plates (Fig 13-4). Pencil label the underside of the base slab and the inside faces of the

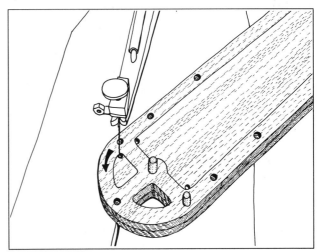

FIGURE 13-3

To pierce a window, unhitch the blade, pass it through a pilot hole, rehitch and retension and start the cut. Reverse the procedure when the window has been fretted out.

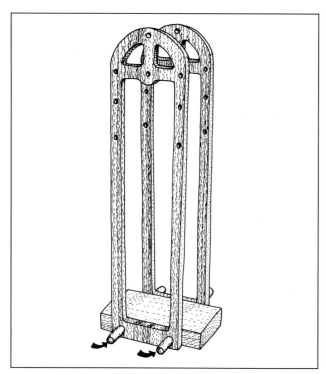

FIGURE 13-4
Have a trial fitting of the two main frames to the base slab.

frames so you can fit everything back in the same position.

MAKING THE ESCAPEMENT

1 Start by looking at the working drawing (Fig 13-1) and template design (Fig 13-2) and noting that the escapement mechanism is made up of three primary components—the toothed wheel, the anchor with the finger pallets and the cord drum—all supported on pivots and rods.

2 Now take your chosen piece of prepared ¾″-thick wood and use the pencil, ruler and compasses to mark the lines that make up the design (Fig 13-2). Draw the two circles—the large outer circle and the inner circle—run 22 equal step-offs around the outer circumference, and then draw radius lines and diagonal lines across the resultant intersections, all as illustrated.

Although it's easy enough to work out with a calculator that each of the 22 step-offs springs from a part-circle angle of 16.3636°, meaning 360 divided by 22 equals 16.3636, it's not so easy to divide up the circle as drawn on the wood. We found that the best procedure is to set the dividers to a guesstimate size and then to fix the size of the step-offs by trial and error.

3 With all the lines carefully drawn, move to the band saw and set to work cutting the teeth. Work at a slow pace, all the while making sure the tooth points occur on the outer circumference (Fig 13-5). Be mindful

that perhaps more than anything else, the success of the movement depends on the length and spacing of the teeth.

4 To make the drum and spacers, swiftly turn the wood down to a 1½″-diameter cylinder, and then use the dividers to step off the guidelines that make up the drum. From right to left along the length of the wood, allow a small amount for tailstock waste, about ¼″ for the first rim, about 1″ for the central area, and another ¼″ for the other rim (Fig 13-6). In fact, the spacing isn't too important, as long as the total length of the drum is as near as possible to 1¼″. Sand the drum to a good finish, and then part off from the lathe.

5 Follow basically the same turning procedures to cut the three spacer drums that hold and distance the anchor on its pivot. Turn down the wood to a

FIGURE 13-5
Cut out the toothed wheel with a series of straight cuts. Make sure the points all occur on the circumference line.

FIGURE 13-6
Use the dividers to check the various step-offs that make up the design.

circumference of about ¾", and run it through with the ¼" bit (Fig 13-7). Cut the two primary spacers to length, and then cut an extra length so you can use additional slices as fine shim adjustments.

6 When you prepare to make the anchor, first have a look at the working drawing (Fig 13-1) and the template design (Fig 13-2), and see that the characteristic asymmetrical profile needs to be cut with a fair degree of precision.

7 Draw the imagery to shape and size, make a tracing, and press transfer the traced lines through to your chosen piece of wood. Have the profile arranged so there is a minimum of fragile short grain at the pallet points. Fix the position of the pivot point, and run it through with the ¼"-diameter drill bit.

FIGURE 13-7
Fit the bit in the tailstock drill chuck, and run the pivot hole through the length of the turning.

8 When you are happy with the image, use the scroll saw to carefully cut out the profile (Fig 13-8).

9 When you have completed all the component parts that make up the escapement—the drum, toothed wheel, anchor and spacers—slide the anchor and spacers in place on their pivot rod, fix the wheel to the drum with a couple of dowel pins, slide the drum rod in place, and have a trial fitting—just so you can see how all the components come together (Fig 13-9).

MAKING THE PENDULUM

1 Have a look at the working drawing (Fig 13-1), and see that the pendulum is made up of two component parts: the disk or whorl, and the long arm. Note how the arm is shaped so that most of the weight occurs at the disk end.

2 Take your chosen length of 1" × 1"-square section wood and turn it down to a smooth, round section.

3 Now take the skew chisel and start turning the spindle to shape. With the spigot and large-diameter end at the headstock end of the lathe, first turn the heavy, round-nosed shape and establish the diameter of the spigot, and then make repeated "downhill" passes to turn the long, slender taper to shape (Fig 13-10).

4 To turn the disk weight, take your chosen 5" × 5"-square slab of wood and then fix the center point by drawing crossed diagonals, scribe out a 4½"-diameter circle, and cut out the blank on the scroll saw.

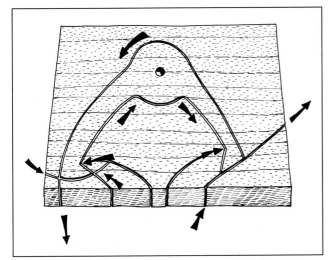

FIGURE 13-8
When you prepare to fret out the anchor escapement on the scroll saw, make sure the line of cut is true to the drawn line, meaning the line of cut is fractional to the waste side of the drawn line.

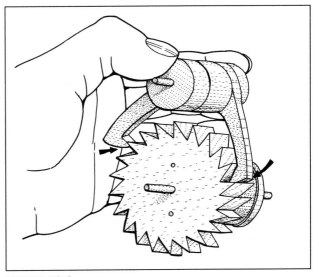

FIGURE 13-9
At every step along the way, stop and make sure the parts come together for a good fit.

FIGURE 13-10
Remove the waste with a long, slow, shaving cut.

FIGURE 13-11
The pendulum weight and the arm. Fit the two together so the grain runs across the width of the disk.

5 Having mounted the wood on the screw chuck and fitted the whole works on the lathe, take the gouge and swiftly turn down the wood to a smooth pill, or disk.

6 Make sure the wood is still secure, and then turn the edges to a nicely rounded profile and rub down the face and edge to a smooth finish.

7 With what is now the back of the pendulum disk, cleanly and crisply turned, remove and refit the workpiece on the screw chuck so the other face is presented, and follow the turning procedures in much the same way as already described. Note that we have given the front of the pendulum a more adventurous profile—a nicely plumped-out front with a dimple at center (Fig 13-11).

8 Finally, when you have what you consider is a strong shape—with all faces and edges being well finished—remove the workpiece from the lathe, and drill a ¼"-diameter spigot hole at top-edge center.

PUTTING TOGETHER AND FINISHING

1 When you have completed all the component parts that make up the project (Fig 13-12), have a trial run and then do the gluing when all the problems have been sorted out.

2 Start by pegging the frames at either side of the base slab, as in our original tryout stage (Fig 13-4).

3 Drill and peg the long spacer cylinder to the front face of the anchor, and test it out for fit and function (Fig 13-13).

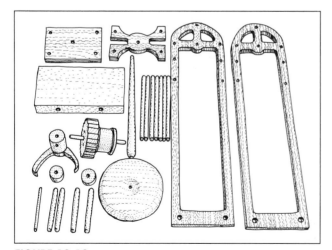

FIGURE 13-12
Set out all the component parts, and check them for possible problems.

FIGURE 13-13
Make sure the toothed wheel and the anchor escapement are carefully and correctly aligned. Check against the working drawing.

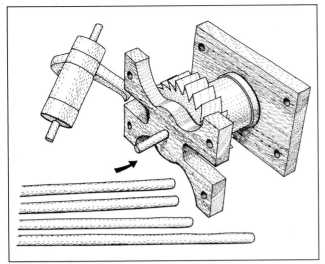

FIGURE 13-14
Gather all the parts that make up the escapement, and make sure they fit and come together nicely.

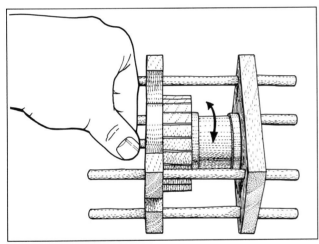

FIGURE 13-15
Set and support the toothed wheel and the drum between the cradle plates, and recheck that the pivot is still free running.

4 Take the two secondary "cradle" plates and the toothed, wheel-and-drum unit, fit the pivot rod, drill the rod holes, and generally make sure it's all going to come together (Fig 13-14).

5 Set the wheel and drum in place—on the pivot rod and in the cradle—and make sure the anchor escapement is smooth and easy on its pivot (Fig 13-15).

6 Having completed the whole escapement unit, take your knife and a fold of fine-grade sandpaper and generally fit and fiddle until all the bearing surfaces move with the minimum of friction (Fig 13-16). Note that the spacer cylinders are used to ensure that the anchor escapement sits over the pallet wheel. You might find you need extra spacers or you need to set the spacers in a

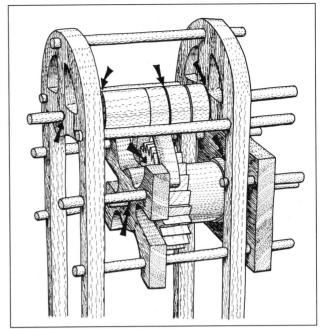

FIGURE 13-16
The bearing faces, meaning the moving faces that rub together, need to be absolutely smooth.

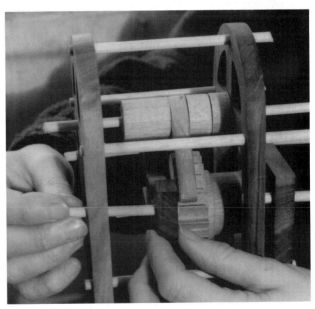

FIGURE 13-17
Set the cradle on its support rods, and adjust the distance between the front slab and the front of the toothed wheel.

different sequence on the pivot rod (Fig 13-17).

7 Now make sure the recoil, or movement, is running smoothly (Fig 13-18).

8 The movement of the anchor escapement in relation to the teeth on the wheel is critical, so spend time making fine adjustments (Fig 13-19).

FIGURE 13-18
Make sure the frames are square and not twisted or skewed.

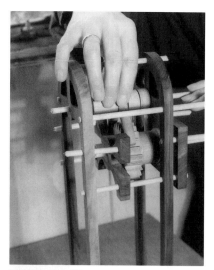

FIGURE 13-19
Ease the movement until the anchor and the toothed wheel move in harmony.

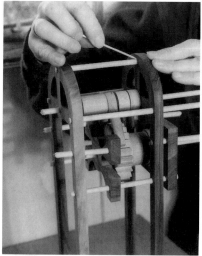

FIGURE 13-20
Use the round toothpicks as temporary holding wedges.

9 You might find it necessary to use the fine-point rounded toothpicks as temporary wedge pins. Set the frames the required distance apart and push the toothpicks in to hold (Fig 13-20).

10 Once you have all the component parts well placed now that the whole machine is up and running, take a fine-toothed saw—or you might use a knife—and mark the length of the fixing rods (Fig 13-21). Allow about 1/16″ extra at each end of the rods so they stand slightly proud of the frame.

11 Have a trial fitting of the pendulum, and cut the arm to length. The pendulum needs to clear the base by about 1/4″. Now is the time to search out a suitable weight and a length of fine, strong cord.

12 When you have had a trial run fitting, cut the various rods and pivots to length, and generally sorted everything out, then disassemble the machine and rebuild using a small amount of PVA adhesive. Finally, burnish the machine with teak oil, fit the cord and the drum weight, and . . . hickory dickory dock, it's time to . . . err . . . try your clock!

PROBLEM SOLVING

■ If you decide to use a different wood, make sure it is strong across the grain. In the context of this project, it's most important you avoid woods that are likely to shrink.
■ The mechanism can only run for a short time, as the weight has a limited fall, or drop. That said, you could modify the design and have a long fall by having the machine hanging on the wall—like a pendulum clock.

FIGURE 13-21
Mark the rod lengths with saw cuts.

PROJECT FOURTEEN

Flywheel and Governor Machine

Color photo page 40

PROJECT BACKGROUND

When I was a kid, I loved fairgrounds and circuses. I was absolutely fascinated by the whirling, twirling balls that could be seen on the traction engines and stationary generators that were used to power the various rides. The governor contraptions looked for all the world like little spinning men holding heavy weights out at arm's length.

The mesmerizing thing was that as the speed of the engine picked up, the little men turned faster and faster, with arms higher and higher, until the weights—usually bright, shiny balls—were being spun around at shoulder height.

In dictionary terms, "a governor is an automatic device designed to regulate the speed of a steam or gasoline en-

gine or other prime mover." As the speed picks up and the spindle spins faster, the centrifugal force of the flyweights being thrown up and out cause the engine to slow down to its assigned speed.

With our little machine, when the cord is swiftly pulled and released, the flywheel is set in motion, with the effect that the two weights fly up and out and cause the flywheel to slow down (above).

PROJECT OVERVIEW

This project requires turning on the lathe (Fig 14-1). You will see that apart from the two spindle-shaft collars, the two linkup arms and the shop-bought dowels, just about everything else is turned on the lathe.

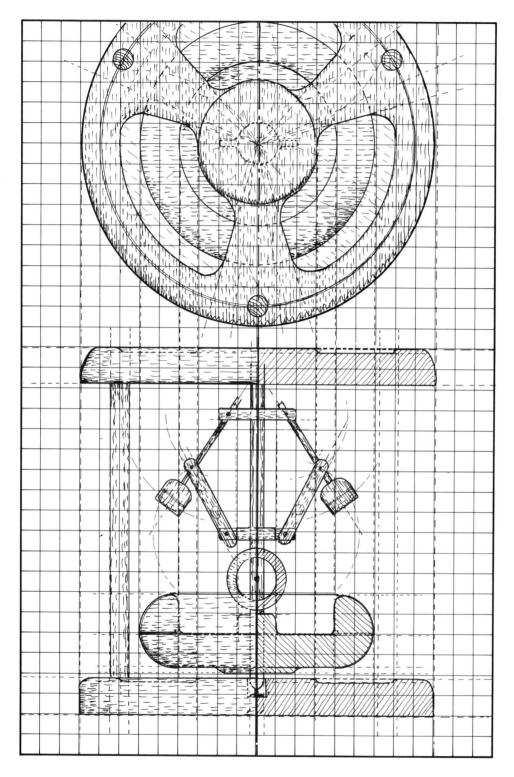

FIGURE 14-1
At a grid scale of two squares to 1", the machine stands about 9" high and 8½" to 9" in diameter.

PROJECT FOURTEEN: TEMPLATE DESIGN

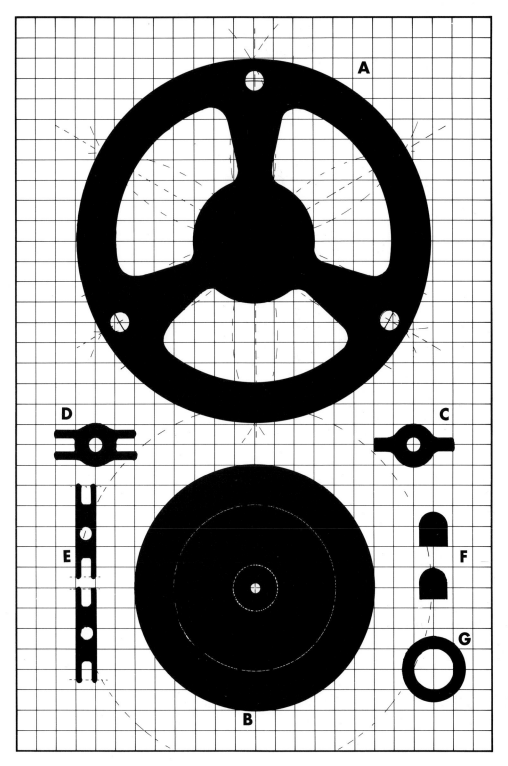

FIGURE 14-2
The scale is two grid squares to 1".
A *Disks (2).*
B *Flywheel.*
C *Male collar.*
D *Female collar.*
E *Linkup arms.*
F *Weights.*
G *Pullcord ring.*

CUTTING LIST—PROJECT FOURTEEN

A Disks (2)	2—1 × 10 × 10 beech
B Flywheel	2 × 7 × 7 sycamore or maple
C Male collar	3/8 × 1 1/4 × 2 1/4 plum
D Female collar	3/8 × 1 1/4 × 2 1/4 plum
E Linkup arms	2—3/8 × 1 × 2 1/2 plum
F Weights	2 × 2 cherry
G Pullcord ring	2 × 2 cherry
Central shaft	white dowel
Support columns (3)	dark wood dowel

CHOOSING YOUR WOOD

As always, when you are choosing wood for turning on the lathe, you need to ask yourself at least three questions: Is the wood easy to turn? Is the wood strong enough for its task? Is the wood suitable in terms of weight, color and texture? Keep these things in mind when choosing wood for the different parts of this project.

MAKING THE TOP AND BASE DISKS

1 Notice when looking at the working drawing (Fig 14-1) and the template design (Fig 14-2) that the two turned disks have more or less the same cross-section profile. They are about 9″ in diameter, with a raised rim and center at about 7/8″ thick and a lowered moat between the rim and center at about 1/8″ deep. Don't struggle too hard to turn two identical disks, because after all, the greater part of the base disk is hidden from view.

2 Begin by taking one of the slabs and fix the center point by drawing crossed diagonals. This done, scribe out a 9″-diameter circle, and cut out the blank on the scroll saw.

3 Screw fix the 9″ blank on the large faceplate so the screws are near the center, mount the whole works on the outboard end of the lathe, and turn down the wood to a smooth-faced, round-edged disk.

4 When you have turned a good disk, take the dividers and mark the three guideline circles that make up the design. Working from the center, you need a 1 1/2″ radius for the central plateau area, a 3 1/2″ radius to set the width of the moat, and a 4″ radius to fix the position of the line on which the three pillars are to be placed.

FIGURE 14-3
Lower the moat area so the rim and the center stand in relief by about 1/8″.

5 Having checked that the lines are correctly placed, lower the moat area by about 1/8″. The raised areas should run in a smooth curve into the moat (Fig 14-3). Mark the center point of the disk.

6 With the first disk made and off the lathe, rerun the whole procedure to make a second disk.

7 With the two disks being more or less the same size, run a 1/16″-diameter hole through the center point, and fit the disks together with a nail or pin so they are placed one on top of another—like a turntable. Make sure the top disk is uppermost.

8 Having first looked at the working drawing (Fig 14-1) and template design (Fig 14-2) and seen how the three posts are set equidistant around the circle, set your dividers so the radius matches the distance from the center point through to the outer-circle guideline, and then pace off around the guideline to make six equal step-offs. Mark every other step-off so the circle is divided into three equal cake-wedge slices (Fig 14-4). This done, use the pencil, ruler and compasses to mark all the other lines that make up the design.

9 With all the guidelines in place, remove the top disk and run the three postholes through with the 1/2″-diameter bit. While you are at it, run a single pilot hole through each of the enclosed windows of waste that make up the design.

10 Set the top disk back on the base disk and use the three postholes you've already drilled to run holes through the bottom disk. The procedure is drill one of the holes on through the bottom disk, fix the position of the hole by pegging it with a dowel, and then complete the other two holes (Fig 14-5).

11 Having drilled the three postholes through both disks, put the base disk to one side, remove the pin, and shade in on the top disk the windows of waste that need to be cut away (Fig 14-6).

12 Move to the scroll saw and fret out the windows of waste. To cut out the enclosed windows, the order of work is:
- Unhitch the scroll saw blade.
- Pass the blade through the pilot hole.
- Refit and retension the blade.
- Cut out the window.
- When you have fretted out one window, reverse the procedure to remove the blade, and move on to the next window to be cut out.

13 After cutting out all three windows, go over the piece lightly with the sandpaper. Now drill two ³⁄₈″-diameter, ½″-deep holes—one down into the center of the base slab and the other up into the center of the underside of the top slab.

TURNING THE FLYWHEEL

1 After looking at the working drawing cross sections (Fig 14-1 bottom right), study the overall shape and profile of the flywheel. Note that although the form is very much like a bowl—it has a rim at the circumference, a slight foot or step-up on the base, and a lowered or sunken area—it also has the addition of a raised dias, or hub, at inside center.

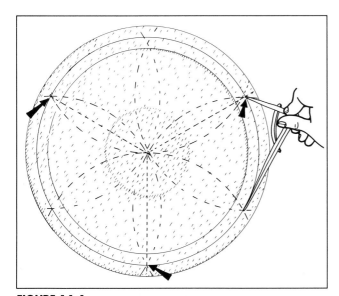

FIGURE 14-4
Set the dividers to the radius of the guideline circle, and step off six equidistant points. Use every other point for the pole holes.

FIGURE 14-5
Tap a dowel through the first hole to hold everything in place, and then drill out the other two holes.

FIGURE 14-6
Mark the shape of the three spokes and the shape of the windows, and shade in the areas that need to be cut away.

FIGURE 14-7
Use the parting tool to clear the bulk of the waste.

2 When you have familiarized yourself with the form, take the 2″-thick slab of wood and follow the marking and cutting procedures as already described. Aim to finish up with a disk blank at about 6½″ in diameter.

3 In sequential order, mount the blank on the screw chuck and then mount the chuck on the lathe so the whole works is safe and secure.

4 Position the tool rest over the bed of the lathe, and set to work turning down the blank to size. The best procedures for setting out a turning of this character are to first run the parting tool straight into the wood to establish the diameter, then true up the face of the disk with the large gouge, and then use the dividers to mark the guidelines. And, of course, along the way, you are swiftly turning off the large areas of waste, so you have to make repeated checks with the calipers. For example, you need to check the overall diameter, the depth from front to back and so on.

5 Having turned down the blank to a diameter of about 6″, marked the 2″-thick edge with a center line, and used the dividers to mark the width of the rim and the diameter of the central hub, use the parting tool to rough out the inside-bowl area. Being sure your tools are razor sharp, run the parting tool straight into the wood to establish the depth and width of the lowered area, and then systematically clear the waste with repeated side-by-side thrusts (Fig 14-7).

6 With the bulk of the waste out of the way, use the tools of your choice to bring the blank to shape. I used the skew chisel and the round-nosed gouge for shaping the curved shoulders and the parting tool for tidying up the back of the turning.

7 Use the wire to burn in the decorative scorch line around the tirelike rim (Fig 14-8) and the sandpaper to bring the turning to a supersmooth finish. If your lathe has a change of direction option, it's best to rub down in both directions of spin.

8 Finally, run a ⅜″-diameter hole through the center of the hub.

TURNING THE FLYWEIGHTS AND PULLCORD RING

1 The flyweight's shape is not too important, as long as they are not so large they clunk into the support posts when they are set in motion. You can use different wood types for these parts.

2 Mount the 2″ × 2″-square section wood between the chuck and the tailstock, and swiftly turn it down to the largest possible diameter. Take the parting tool and the calipers and reduce a 3″ length at the tailstock end to a diameter of between ¾″ to ⅞″.

3 Use the dividers to set out the step-offs that make up the design. Working from the tailstock end, allow about ½″ for the tailstock waste, ⅜″ each for the two halves of the first weight, ⅜″ for the between-weight waste, two more ⅜″ step-offs for the second weight, and another ½″ for waste.

4 Use the parting tool to sink the waste. Run the tool straight in so you are left with a central core at about ½″ diameter. Use the toe of the skew chisel to cut in the decorative midlines (Fig 14-9).

5 Now use the skew chisel to turn off the round shoulders at the top of the weights. Being mindful that the two turnings need to be identical, it's best to turn off the shapes little by little so they are looking at each other and the mirror imaged. If you take a slice off the left-hand shoulder and then a little off the right-hand shoulder and so on, backward and forward, you are more

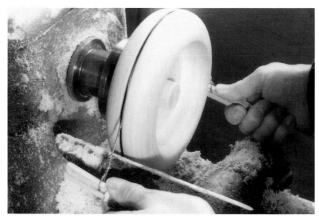

FIGURE 14-8
Hold the cutting wire so you can swiftly let go of the stick handles if the wire snags.

FIGURE 14-9
Use the toe of the skew chisel to cut in the midlines.

FIGURE 14-10
The best way of achieving a well-matched pair of forms is to work them as a mirror-image profile.

likely to achieve two well-matched turnings.

6 Having turned off the round shoulders on both turnings (Fig 14-10), use the fine-grade sandpaper to rub down the whole workpiece to a smooth finish, and then part off with a fine-toothed saw.

7 One piece at a time, mount the little turnings in the four-jaw chuck so they are gripped by their stalks of waste, and use the skew chisel to turn down the shouldered end to a smooth, rounded finish (Fig 14-11).

8 While the workpiece is still held in the four-jaw chuck, set the drill chuck in the tailstock end of the lathe, and drill the turning through with a ¼"-diameter bit (Fig 14-12). Lastly, take the turning off the lathe, and rub down the flat end to a smooth finish. Rerun this procedure for the other turning.

9 Having turned off the two flyweights, remount the other end of the turned cylinder in the lathe—or you might be using another length of wood—and set to work turning off the pull cord ring.

10 With the wood turned down to a diameter of 1½", set the dividers to ½" and mark all the step-offs that make up the design. The best procedure is to set out four ½" step-offs, one at each end for waste and two at the center for the ring.

11 When the guide cuts are in place, take the skew chisel and swiftly bring the wood to shape. It's a simple procedure; all you do is lower the waste at each end, cut in the decorative midline, and then round over the shoulders.

12 When you are satisfied with the basic ring shape, fit the drill chuck in the tailstock mandrel, set a 1"-diameter Forstner bit in the drill, and run a hole all the way through the turning (Fig 14-13). Be careful not to force the pace or in any way do damage to the bit or the turning. The easiest method is to advance the bit a little, then withdraw, then wind back some more and so on until you reach the desired depth. Warning: If you try to force the bit through in one great thrust, you are likely to burn the drill or split the wood. This done, back the drill bit out of the way, sand down the turning to a smooth finish and then part off. Finally, drill a ½"-diameter hole through the ring—in one side and out the other.

MAKING THE COLLAR RINGS AND LINKUP ARMS

1 Look at the working drawing (Fig 14-1), the template design (Fig 14-2), and the various project photographs. There are two collars on the central shaft: a fixed female collar at the top and a sliding male collar at the bottom. The female collar is designed in such a way

FIGURE 14-11
Secure the weight in the jaws of the chuck, and alternately use the skew chisel and sandpaper to achieve a smooth, round-topped finish.

FIGURE 14-12
Run the hole through with the ¼"-diameter drill bit. Having the bit held in the tailstock drill chuck ensures that the hole is perfectly placed.

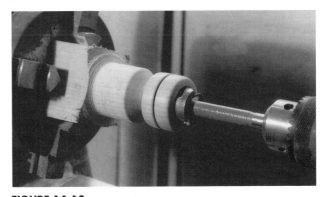

FIGURE 14-13
If you cut the neck of waste at a smaller core diameter than the diameter of the through-hole, the ring should come away clean as you complete the hole.

that its mortiselike flanges receive the end of a dowel, while the male collar is designed so its tenon fits into the female flange at the end of the linkup arm. Note that the two collars are more or less identical.

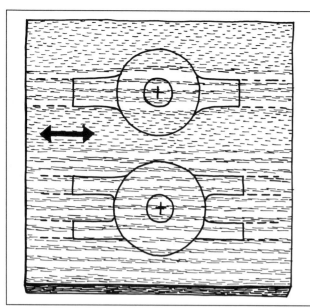

FIGURE 14-14
Use the pencil, ruler and dividers/compasses to mark the shape of the two collars. Note the direction of the grain.

2 When you have a clear understanding of how the two collars function, use the pencil, ruler and compasses to mark them on your chosen piece of hard, close-grained, knot-free ⅜″-thick wood (Fig 14-14). Note that the designs need to be marked so the flanges are aligned with the run of the grain.

3 Still using the pencil, ruler and compasses, and still working on the ⅜″-thick wood, mark the shape of the two identical linkup arms.

4 Move to the drill press and run the collars through with a ⅜″-diameter hole at the center.

5 Move to the scroll saw, and fret out the profiles. As you are cutting out the flanges, make sure they are a loose fit one within another.

6 When you have completed the four cutouts, sand the various flanges and extensions so they are nicely smoothed and rounded (Fig 14-15).

7 When you have completed the four cutouts, go back to the drill press and drill with ¹⁄₁₆″-diameter holes at all the pivot points (Fig 14-16). Lastly, drill a single fixing hole through the top collar so it runs across the shaft hole, and then run as many weight-reducing holes through the linkarms as necessary.

PUTTING TOGETHER AND FINISHING

1 When you have completed all the component parts that make up the project (Fig 14-17)—the base and

FIGURE 14-15
Use the rotary tool to bring all the corners and edges to a nicely rounded finish.

FIGURE 14-16
See to it that the depth of the joint is adequate.

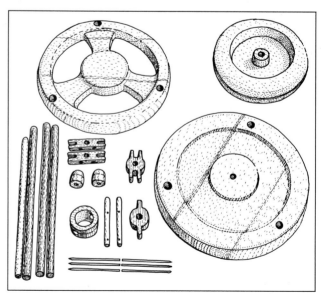

FIGURE 14-17
Spread all the component parts out on the work surface, and check them against your working drawing and template design.

top disks, flywheel, three poles, two linkup arms, two flyweights, two collars, two ¼″ rods that make up the upper arms and pull cord ring—set them on the work surface and check them over for potential problems. Then comes the fun stage of the first fitting.

2 Having first looked at the working drawing (Fig 14-1 bottom center) and seen how the main shaft is pivoted on a little pin-and-tack bearing, tap a brass pin or nail into the bottom of the main shaft, and push a brass thumbtack into the base hole.

3 With the base slab flat on the bench, tap the three poles in place, slide the main shaft through the flywheel, and set the bottom end of the shaft in the center-of-base bearing hole (Fig 14-18). The shaft should be a tight push fit through the wheel, with the bottom of the end protruding about ⅜″ or so from the underside.

4 When you have eased the bottom of the shaft with a scrap of fine-grade sandpaper so it's a smooth fit in the bearing hole, slide the pull cord ring and the two collars in position (Fig 14-19). See to it that the ring and the male collar are a loose, easy-sliding fit.

5 With the ring and the two collars in place, rub down six round toothpicks and then tackle one joint at a time. It's all simple enough, as long as you bear in mind that the joints need to be smooth and easy, with the pivot pins being a tight fit through the two outermost holes and a loose fit through the innermost hole. Continue one joint at a time, easing, adjusting and pencil labeling so you can repeat the correct arrangement the second time around (Fig 14-20).

6 When all the joints are loose and easy, and when you have established the full extent of the rise and fall of the arms, slide the flyweights in place, and mark their position with pencil registration marks (Fig 14-21).

7 With the trial fitting complete and the various holes marked and drilled, disassemble the machine and rerun the sequence, this time gluing all the dowel and pin joints.

8 Finally, rub down any rough dowel/pin ends, drill the pull string hole, give the whole works a generous wipe with the teak oil, cut a pull string, and . . . wonderful—the machine is ready for action.

PROBLEM SOLVING
- When attaching the base and top blanks to the large faceplate, don't place the screws too near the edge rim.
- Use a strong, thin cord for the pull string.

FIGURE 14-18
Ease the bearing hole and the end of the shaft so the whole component spins like a top.

FIGURE 14-19
Slide the ring and the collars in place on the shaft. The top collar needs to be a tight fit.

FIGURE 14-20
Make constant checks to ensure that every joint is a good fit.

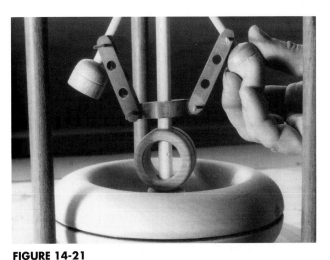

FIGURE 14-21
Make sure the flyweights don't in any way restrict the movement of the arms or the circumference of swing.

Cam Machine

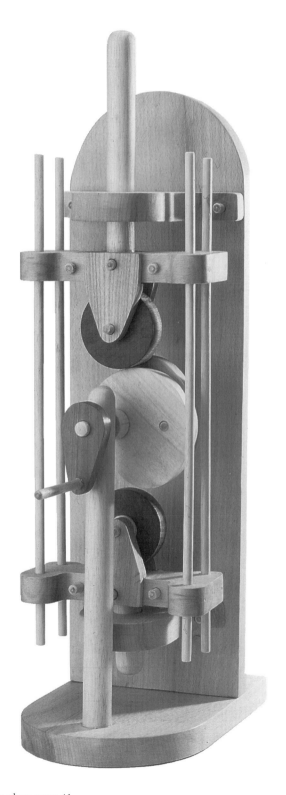

Color photo page 41

PROJECT BACKGROUND

It's not simply that the movement is extra difficult or the design is ultracomplex or the techniques are more complicated than the other projects; it's all of these and then some!

As the encyclopedia so rightly says, "a cam is a part of a machine, or mechanism, used for transforming rotary or oscillating motion by direct sliding or rolling contact into any prescribed motion of a second part known as a follower." Or, to put it another way, a cam is a rotating cylinder or plate with an irregular profile attached to a revolving shaft to give a reciprocating motion to a part in contact with it.

Cams are to be found primarily in machinery where automatic control and timing are part of the operation. In simple terms, when a cam revolves on its shaft, another mechanism, called a follower, stays in close physical contact with the cam profile, with the effect that its movement reflects that of the cam. For example, if we have a true wheel on a shaft, and if we have one end of a seesaw pressing down on the wheel rim, it's plain to see that the turning movement of the wheel will have little or no effect on the seesaw. But, then again, if the wheel has a bulge or a stud set into its rim, then every time the revolving bump or peg comes into contact with the seesaw, the seesaw will jolt up and down. The predictable jolt-jolt-jolt action is the mechanical happening that turns the wheel-and-seesaw apparatus into a cam and follower.

Our machine is a disk cam with rollers. The working action is simple and direct: As the crank handle is turned, the two plate cams are set in motion and the wheels follow the cams, with the effect that the frame and the shafts bob up and down (left).

PROJECT OVERVIEW

Although there is no denying this project is a challenge, the challenging aspect has more to do with being able to "see" the machine in your mind's eye and successfully putting the parts together so the machine works than with being able to perform overly complex or complicated woodworking techniques.

It's important to note that the success or failure of the machine depends almost entirely on the two cam plates being accurately cut and placed. The cams have to be spot on.

PROJECT FIFTEEN: WORKING DRAWING

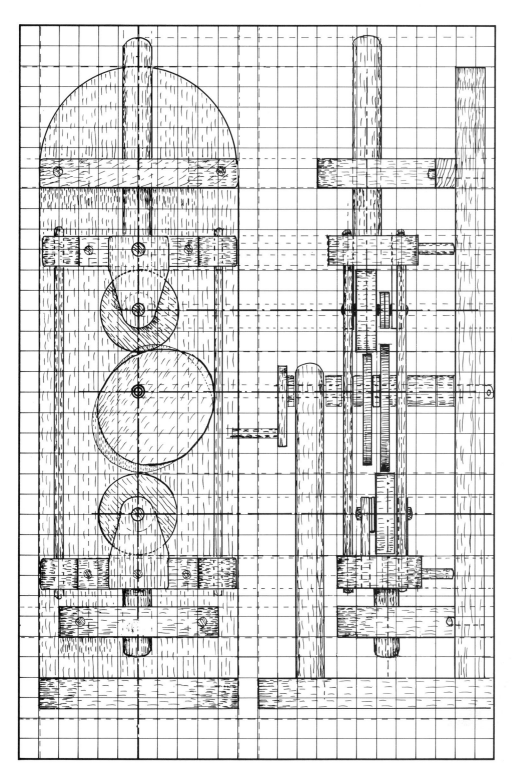

FIGURE 15-1
At a grid scale of two squares to 1", the machine stands about 15½" high and 5" wide.

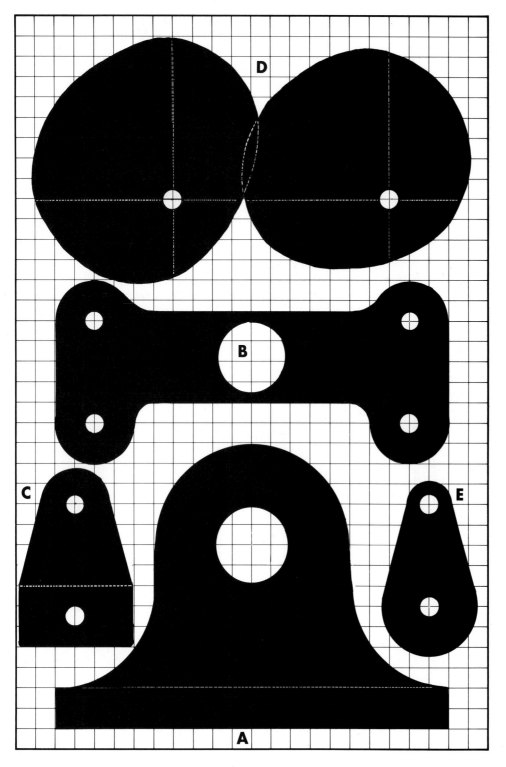

FIGURE 15-2
The scale is four grid squares to 1".
A *Brackets.*
B *Chassis plates.*
C *Wheel plates (4).*
D *Cams.*
E *Crank.*

CUTTING LIST—PROJECT FIFTEEN

A	Brackets	2—¾ × 3½ × 5 beech
B	Chassis plates	2—¾ × 2¼ × 5 beech
C	Wheel plates (4)	³⁄₁₆ × 1½ × 20 cherry
D	Cams	2—¼ × 3¼ × 3¼ tulip
E	Crank	¼ × 1¼ × 2¼ plum
	Backboard	¾ × 5 × 16 beech
	Base	¾ × 5 × 8 beech
	Pegs, rods, shafts and pins	¾″ white wood dowel
	Follow wheels	2¼ × 2¼ × 6 walnut

CHOOSING YOUR WOOD

As this machine needs be made with a high degree of accuracy, it's all the more important your chosen wood be hard, straight grained, easy to work, and free from knots, warps and splits. The wood needs to be stable and predictable. With these factors uppermost in our mind, we decided at the outset to use European beech for the base, backboard, and just about all the bits and pieces in between; cherry for the wheel plates; American walnut for the two follower wheels; plum for the crank plate; a nice piece of tulip for the two cam plates; and carefully selected white wood dowel for all the pegs, rods, shafts and pins.

MAKING THE BASE, BACK AND BRACKETS

1 When you have studied the working drawing (Fig 15-1), the template design (Fig 15-2), and all the hands-on photographs, use the pencil, ruler, compasses and square to mark the shape and profile of the base, back slabs and two brackets. Make sure the grain runs along the length of the back and base slabs and from front to back through the brackets.

2 With the shapes carefully drawn, then comes the task of fretting them out. No problem with the back and base slabs—all you do is run the line of cut around the drawn line and the job is done—but the brackets are a little more complicated. The easiest procedure for cutting the two brackets is pin the two slabs of wood together, bore them through with the ⅞″ to ¾″-diameter bit, slide a length of suitable dowel in your chosen hole size, and fret them out on the scroll saw.

3 After cutting out the two brackets (Fig 15-3), pencil label one "top" and the other "bottom." Take the "bottom" bracket, draw in the line as shown (Fig 15-2

FIGURE 15-3

To ensure a good profile and accurate hole alignment, pin the two slabs together, and have a length of dowel running through the two holes. You will need to keep a tight hold when the blade exits at the end of the cut when the two pinned areas of waste have been more or less cut away.

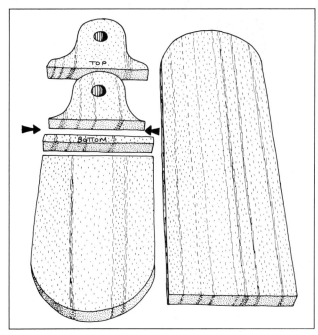

FIGURE 15-4

The four large component parts—the base, backboard and two brackets—showing a slice cut away from the bottom bracket.

bottom), and slice off the strip with the saw (Fig 15-4).

4 If all is well, when you place the brackets in position on the backboard, the shaft holes should be misaligned or offset by the thickness of the strip of waste you've just cut away. When you are pleased that all is correct, sand down all four cutouts—the base, back and two brackets—to a smooth, round-edged finish.

MAKING THE FOLLOWER WHEEL BOGEYS

1 If you look at the working drawing (Fig 15-1), template design (Fig 15-2) and various hands-on photographs, you will see that the two wheels that follow the cam, called follower wheels, are each held and contained in a frame, or bogey, that is made up primarily from a long, bone-shaped chassis and two shield-shaped wheel plates. If you further study the designs, you will see that although each bogey is made up of an identical chassis cutout, the top wheel chassis is arranged so that it is offset from the bottom wheel chassis. The big, end bulges on the top chassis face the backboard, while the big bulges on the bottom chassis face front.

2 Take the wood you have selected for the two bogey chassis plates, pin and drill them as already described for the brackets, and then fret them out on the scroll saw (Fig 15-5).

3 With the two identical chassis plates crisply cut out and finished, set them flat on the surface so the big-bulge ends are looking toward each other, and pencil label them for swift identification. If you look to the two cutouts shown (Fig 15-6), best label the one in the foreground "top" and the other one "bottom."

4 Now take the wood pieces you have set aside for the wheel plates and stack, pin, drill and dowel them in much the same way as already described so you have a single eight-layer stack.

5 Take the eight-layer stack—with the design drawn on the top layer and the dowels in place—and run them through on the scroll saw so you have eight identical cutouts. Divide the cutouts into two stacks of four, and cut a strip from one stack (Fig 15-7).

6 You should now have four complete shield shapes, each with two holes; four strips, each with a single hole; and four triangle shapes, each with a single hole (Fig 15-8). Set the four strips aside (two of these are used at a later stage), pair the one-hole plates up with the two-hole plates so bottom holes are aligned, and glue them together as shown (Fig 15-8).

FIGURE 15-5
Having the holes drilled and all the dowels set in place—all prior to cutting—is the best way of making sure you finish up with two identical cutouts.

FIGURE 15-6
Set the two cutouts flat so they are reversed and you know what goes where and how.

FIGURE 15-7
Group the wheel plates in two stacks of four, set the dowels in place through one stack, and run that stack through on the scroll saw.

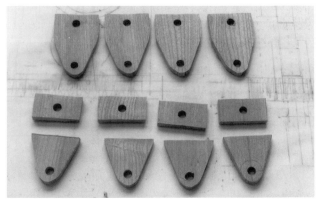

FIGURE 15-8
Pair up the cutouts for best fit, and put the waste strips to one side. One pair of plates at a time, smear glue on mating faces, make sure the holes are well aligned, and put the plates to one side until the glue is dry.

MAKING THE FOLLOWER WHEELS AND DOWEL-SLICE WASHERS

1 Look at the working drawing (Fig 15-1).

2 Mount a piece of 2¼″ × 2¼″ walnut on the lathe.

3 With the wood in place on the lathe, take your gouge and turn down the wood to the largest possible diameter. Now take the skew chisel and the calipers and carefully skim the wood to a 2″ cylinder. Be precise.

4 Starting at the tailstock end, use the ruler and dividers to mark the cylinder with the step-offs: a small amount for tailstock waste, ½″ for the first wheel, ⅜″ for parting waste, ½″ for the second wheel, ⅜″ for parting waste, and the remainder for another project.

5 Take the parting tool and sink the waste to a depth of about ¾″, so you are left with a central core at about ½″ (Fig 15-9).

6 On the lathe, drill a ¼″-diameter hole through the length of the project (Fig 15-10). It's a straightforward procedure, as long as you advance and withdraw the drill in a series of small steps. Run the drill in to a depth of about ¼″, then draw it back to clear the waste, then sink the hole another ¼″, then withdraw and clear the waste and so on until the hole is complete.

7 Once you are satisfied with the finished dimensions of the wheels, use the parting tool to part off the wheels.

8 Sand down the part-off faces of the wheel to a smooth finish.

9 Now take the large-diameter dowel you set aside for the washer, drill it through with a ¼″-diameter hole, and slice it off like salami so you have a selection of varying sized washers.

PUTTING TOGETHER AND FINISHING

1 The best procedure is to first dry build with the tight-push pegs, pencil label the whole works with registration marks, and then, when you are sure all is correct, begin gluing and pegging it together (Fig 15-11).

2 Familiarize yourself with how the project fits together. Now mark out the base, back and two brackets. This done, and having first drilled the dowel-fixing holes, dry fit the parts in position, and drive the dowel pegs home.

FIGURE 15-9
Having turned down the wood to a well-finished cylinder and stepped off the thickness of the wheels and the areas of part-off waste, clear the bulk of the waste with the parting tool.

FIGURE 15-10
Run the axle holes through with the ¼″ drill bit.

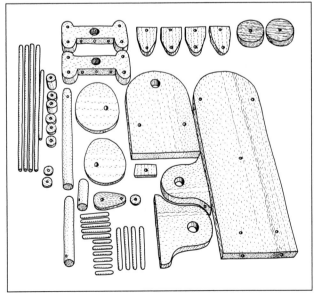

FIGURE 15-11
Set out all the component parts, rub them down to a good finish, and spend time making sure you haven't made any mess-ups. Cut all the rods, dowels and pegs to size.

3 Take the chassis plates, shaft stubs, wheel plates and wheels—all smoothly sanded down and pencil marked—and peg them together. Don't forget to have the wooden washer to one side of the wheel so the wheel is offset in the chassis (Fig 15-12). If you look to the working drawing (Fig 15-1), you will see that with the top wheel, the washer is at the back so the wheel is pushed forward, while with the bottom wheel, the washer is set at the front so the wheel is pushed toward the backboard.

4 Once the wheels and the washers are in place, set the wheel plates firmly in position, and hold the unit secure with the dowel and axle pegs (Fig 15-13). If you've got it right, the push-fit pegs should just about hold everything in place. While you are working on the chassis bogeys, set the distance dowels through the width of the chassis and set them so they relate to the brackets and the backboard. If you look at the working drawing (Fig 15-1), the template drawing (Fig 15-2) and the various photographs, you will see that the function of the distance dowels is to hold the chassis plate a set distance away from the backboard, while at the same time stopping the wheel frame from twisting.

5 With the two bogey carriages complete, slide them in place in the brackets, and set the drive shaft support post in place at the front of the baseboard (Fig 15-15).

6 Move the support post and set the four frame dowels in place so the two bogeys are linked, spaced and aligned (Fig 15-16). With the frame dowels fitted, ease the distance dowels so the whole follower frame slides smoothly up and down in the bracket holes (Fig 15-14).

7 To fit the cams, slide the two cam plates in place on the drive shaft dowel so they are held apart with a suitably thick washer—I use one of the slices cut from the wheel plates. Set the dowel-slice washer at front and back of the cam plates (Fig 15-17), and set the whole component part in place so it is pivoted between the backboard and the support post. And, of course, if you need more or fewer washers, thinner slices or whatever, now is the time to prepare them.

8 When you have played around with the arrangement of dowel-slice washers until the two cams are aligned with the follower wheels, and when you have popped the dowel peg through the two cams so they are linked and held together, spend time adjusting the two wheel bogeys on their four frame shafts so the follower wheels are in contact with the edges of the cams

FIGURE 15-12
Fit the wheel plate on the side of the chassis, slide the axle rod in place, and set the distance washer on the axle.

FIGURE 15-13
Set the wheel plates firmly in position, and hold the unit secure with the dowel pegs and axle. Then pencil label the pieces.

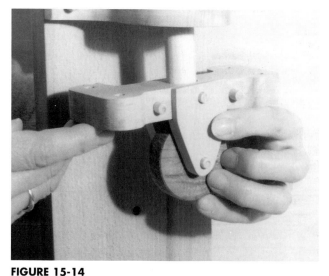

FIGURE 15-14
The distance rods need to be a tight push fit through the width of the chassis and set so the whole bogey is able to freely slide up and down in the bracket hole.

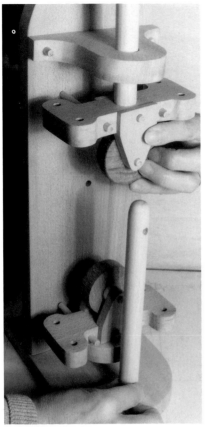

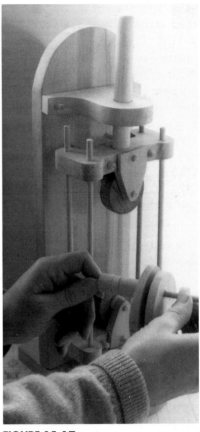

FIGURE 15-15
Set the shaft support pole in place in readiness for the final fitting.

FIGURE 15-16
Slide the four frame dowels in place.

FIGURE 15-17
With the cam plates on the drive shaft, test the movement with washers.

(Fig 15-18). Although you do have to do your best to achieve a good fit and finish to the whole machine, I think you also have to accept compromises. For example, if the wheel pivots are slightly askew, you might have to ease one or other of the parts with the sandpaper.

9 When you have achieved a smooth working action with the frame being neatly lifted up and down by the cams, and when you have labeled the whole machine with as many registration marks as you think necessary, now is the time to glue it up.

10 Finish the project with a rubbing of teak oil.

PROBLEM SOLVING
■ This is one of those wonderfully flexible machines that is open to all sorts of exciting design changes and modifications. For example, you could use it to drive one of the other projects, you could make it bigger or smaller, you could have the chassis bogeys running on tracks, you could have more cams and more follower wheels, you could redesign the frame so that it is held horizontally and so on.

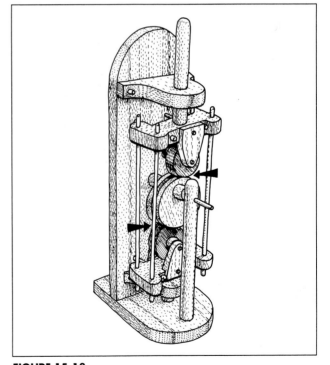

FIGURE 15-18
Add washer slices until each plate is aligned with its follower wheel. You'll need to spend time sanding and adjusting for best fit.

INDEX